Scuppers
to
Skipper

Life in the Royal Navy 1934 - 1958

W.P. Edney

CONTENTS

FOREWORD

Walter P. Edney was a remarkable man. He came from a very humble background and joined the Royal Navy at the lowest possible rank, barely more than a boy. Through the next 25 years, including World War II and the Korean War he rose to become an officer and commander of his own ship. It was rare in those days for men to cross the divide from seaman to officer. In the late 1950's he left the Navy and started his career anew as a repair man for dishwashers, driving to people's homes in a little van. He again rose to become the National Service manager for Colston Ltd. in the UK.

In the early 1990's my father, Walter P Edney, gave me a sheaf of handwritten pages explaining that it was his memoirs. He had spent the last year writing and now asked if I could make it into a book. We typed in the entire set, fascinated by the many details of his life that we had not known before. Eventually this was put into book form with the title (as requested by WPE) of "Fortune without Fame". This was in two parts, the first being his life in the Navy and the second his subsequent civilian life. Part one is a fascinating personal account of life in the Royal Navy though all ranks from the 1930's to the 1950's and it is this account that is published here. Part two is necessarily more personal and of less historical interest and is not included.

Walter P Edney died in 2003 not long after the death of his wife Thelma to whom he was devoted. It is clear that his memoirs were written from detailed diaries. However, no diaries were found after his death from which we assume he destroyed them after writing the memoirs.

He remained a humble man throughout but was, at the same time, a superb leader having the reputation of being hard but scrupulously fair and a man of the highest integrity.

Jonathan Edney, 2015

1 EARLY LIFE

I was born at Leigh on Sea, Essex on 15th October 1918, of somewhat humble parentage. My mother was in domestic service, presumably as a housekeeper, to a Mr. E.B. Walling and my father was a private in the army, stationed at Shoeburyness; the First World War had another month to run.

It always seemed to me that my mother had seen better times. She had been brought up in Amberley, Sussex and appeared to be reasonably well educated. She had four sisters and one brother. Their maiden name was Greenfield. The eldest sister, having married well to a Compton, lived in a rather nice home in Brentwood, Essex, taking in the youngest daughter who never married. Another daughter married less well; the fourth married a station master by the name of West and lived in Mitcham, Surrey. The son, who became a Southern Railway guard, married and lived in Croydon. I am at a loss to know why this family became so scattered or how my mother found herself at Leigh on Sea.

Their original home had been "Hollies" in Amberley which also served as a shop bearing a notice over the door: "Tea, tobacco, snuff and funerals furnished". My mother's father and grandfather were carpenters who made church pews and coffins. Her grandmother, a Mrs. Cain, seemed to be a general factotum of the village and apparently had a will of iron and nerves of steel. She once held a man's arm which had been injured in a shooting accident whilst the doctor amputated it. She was also a midwife.

Walter aged four

Of my father I know little. His family of four brothers and one sister lived at Felpham near Bognor Regis. I never knew my grandfather and only vaguely remember my grandmother. They were agricultural workers with little education. My father could not nor ever did, write a letter. The boys (father & brothers) made little progress in life; two of them continued with work on the land. My Uncle Bill was a sight for sore eyes, cycling around Bognor on a bike laden, front and back with garden produce and dressed rather more roughly and shabbily than a vagrant. My father found employment at the local gas works stoking coal to make gas whilst the younger brother was also employed there as a crane driver. The daughter married an agricultural worker and lived first near Fareham and subsequently at Merrow near Guildford.

I presume that I was born at the home of Mr. E.B. Walling, a gentleman that I cannot recall ever meeting but who was affectionately known to me as "Uncle Ernie" and with whom I communicated until after my marriage. Certainly, I remember that he never failed to send me nice presents on my birthday and at Christmas. I still have a book that he sent me in 1923 called "Everyland", full of stories from around the world including one written by himself on the attempt by Scott to conquer Mount Everest. Within one year of my birth we moved from Leigh on Sea to Bognor.

This early pattern of moving may well be responsible for my continued moving throughout my life. Who knows! Presumably my father was demobilized, the first war having come to a conclusion on November 11th 1918. My father had then to find employment and felt the best chance of doing so would be back in his home town of Bognor. We took furnished rooms in part of a house at South Bersted and my Father found employment as mentioned earlier, at the Gas Works.

My father's job entailed shovelling coal into a furnace from which the gas was extracted as it burned. Once the gas had been extracted and before the coal was burned through, it was taken from the furnace and sprayed with water to produce coke, subsequently sold for domestic use. It was hard, very hot and dirty work. He would come home, black as a coal miner and bathe in a tin bath. He worked six days a week on alternate shift work, from 6am to 2pm for a week, then 2pm until l0pm followed by the night shift from l0pm to 6am. For this he received the princely sum of £2-10-0 (£2.50) per week or £3 for the night shift. He continued with this work until he was forced to retire with ill health shortly before he was sixty. Needless to say his ill health was caused by the work - constantly breathing in coal dust which damaged his lungs. Compensation was unheard of in those days.

We must have lived in the furnished accommodation for about 2 years, whilst our name was on the Council housing list and in 1921 were allotted a council home. These were terraced homes rapidly built and known as homes for heroes (war heroes). They were constructed of wood with a slate roof and consisted of one parlour/sitting-room/dining-room and one kitchen downstairs. The doors were of thin tongued/groove such as present day shed doors. Off the kitchen was a bathroom with just an enamelled bath, but no taps for water and a copper with a fuel fire underneath for heating the water. The procedure was to fill the copper with cold water by bucket from the kitchen sink, light the fire to heat the water and, when hot, transfer it by bucket to the bath. The copper also served to boil up water in which dirty clothes were washed. Over the bath, on a thick plank was a mangle with large 6" (15cm) wooden rollers and a large turning wheel. Also off the kitchen was a coal cellar and a pantry. The toilet was outside across the back yard - mighty cold it was in winter, when the cistern would freeze

4

up frequently.

Upstairs, there were just three bedrooms, the front being the largest with a medium and small bedroom to the rear. Literally, a "two down and three up residence". There was no electricity but the parlour had a central gas lamp, fitted with a mantle and one gas lamp of a similar nature in the kitchen. No lights upstairs, we used candles for going to bed in the dark. Cooking was by a primitive gas stove whilst a range was fitted in the parlour to give some heat to the room and heat an oven. No hot water was available other than that which could be heated in the copper or on the gas stove and there was no wash basin. Our ablutions were carried out in the sink or, for visitors, we took up a large pitcher of hot water so that they could wash in the earthenware bowl in the front bedroom.

We dined around a table in the centre of the parlour but as this room was no more than 12ft by 10ft (4m by 3m) there was little room for other furniture - though I seem to remember a three-seater settee along one wall and a piano along another. Subsequently, in the mid-1920s electricity was supplied to the road and to our house which made life much more comfortable and we were able to have lights upstairs. There were no power points, but in those days there were few electrical appliances anyway.

In July of 1921 my brother, Bernard, was born. I have no recollection of this, being only 2 years and nine months. Whether my mother had him at home, or went away I know not. Nor who may have looked after father and I during that period or even whether we were in furnished rooms or our house at that date. My earliest recollections are of heating a poker to red hot in the fire, placing it on the hearth and my baby brother sitting on it - bare bottom of course.

I remember starting school before the age of five at Lyon Street Council School in, I think, the pre-infants class but where I certainly learnt my letters and made a start on my multiplication tables. I also remember an occasion when I was staying with my Uncle Henry in Croydon. I do not remember how I got there or returned but none of my immediate family was with me. Uncle Henry had in his home the very latest invention of which he was very proud - a wireless set (radio). It was probably a "cat's whisker" as I doubt

Walter and Bernard

thermionic valves had yet been invented. I do know, that even at that tender age, I was seized with curiosity and when I was alone in the room could not resist lifting the lid and investigating inside. Needless to say, when next my uncle tried to switch on the set, it would not work. Whether or not he ever did get it to work again I shall never know, nor whether he suspected my meddling - but he must have been mighty suspicious.

Another occasion that stands out in my memory is of walking out of school one sunny afternoon and trotting along a long narrow pathway to my grandmother's at Felpham. I don't know why I did this other than perhaps I felt I had had enough of school for that day, but it caused some consternation at the school when it was discovered that I was missing and no one knew where I had gone. My recollection is that I was staying at my grandmother's at the time as my mother was in hospital for an operation.

After the age of five certain memories come back to me. Of one thing I am certain, I was not the easiest child for my mother or anyone else to handle. I was self-willed, determined, stubborn and probably very naughty. My mother did not enjoy good health, to put it mildly. She suffered from chronic asthma and, at times, was literally fighting for breath. For relief she burned "Potter's Asthma Cure" under her nose but that seems to have been the extent of her treatment. With that disability and a difficult child like myself to handle, it is not surprising that frequently she was at her wits end. Smacking me seemed to have little effect - I do not ever remember that she did, but must have done. What I do remember is being threatened with the Lavant Home - a home for delinquent children not far from Midhurst, Sussex. In desperation she would tell me that no longer could she cope with me and had sent for the policeman to take me off to the Lavant Home. I was frightened by this and would stand at the window watching for the policeman to arrive and promising my mother that I would behave in future. He never came of course, nor did I behave in the future.

THE FORMATIVE YEARS

The period between 1924 and 1931, whilst I was aged 6 to 13 were, to say the least, a very difficult period for the country politically, economically and socially. The country was suffering the results of a devastating war, with massive debts to the U.S.A. for the assistance they had given. Consequently, money was in short supply except for the wealthy, who hung on to what they had; unemployment was rife. Industry had not recovered from their war efforts, exports were low and imports, not affordable. This all led to the fact that those who were in employment had to accept wage cuts. Those not in employment received 10 shillings (50p) per week state benefit. The coal miners refused to accept a wage cut and were backed by other unions; a general strike of all workers took place. It did not last long because it meant starvation for those on strike, but was enough to stir the Government into action.

There is no doubt that we were a poor family, although I did not think so at the time. I knew and associated with children of much poorer families than ourselves and so had the feeling that we were better placed than many. We could certainly hold our heads with the average. My father was never out of work and never owed anyone a penny. On the other hand there was never a penny he could fall back on in case of emergency. As far as I know we always lived well. I never went hungry; meat was cheap and plentiful at something like two shillings (10p) for a large joint of beef or lamb. My father grew all of our vegetables, potatoes, peas, carrots, beans, cabbage,

Bernard & Walter 1928

onions etc. so these were plentiful. Cheese, meat-paste, jam was available and dripping (pork fat) on bread was quite a favourite. Bread was t'pence-ha'penny (1p) per loaf. My mother made delicious puddings, roly-poly or in a basin with huge pieces of suet in them - this was pure fat straight from the meat and chopped by hand. I had a dessert spoonful of cod liver oil and malt daily and plenty of Brimstone treacle, whatever that was, but I kept healthy and cannot remember any illness other than the odd turn of influenza when I was fed with a thick onion porridge which I liked and which seemed a good cure. Doctors were only called for serious illnesses as they had to be paid for their services and there was little money for such luxuries. My mother needed the doctor's attention on occasions; her health was not good and her asthma aggravated matters. The doctor would only charge a small amount for such visits and presumably made his money from those who could afford it.

As children, my brother and I were always reasonably well clothed and always well shod. I know not from where our clothes were obtained. I do remember a small Scotsman who would call on Monday evenings to collect money for clothes. I think it was about two shillings (10p). He would sometimes give me a small silver threepenny piece; probably that is why I remember him. Some of my school friends were not so fortunate, their clothes were well worn and I remember one family (Brooks by name) who came to school in clogs because they could not afford shoes.

Our furniture for the house was, in general, purchased from the sale rooms where from time to time auctions were held. I can remember going with my mother to view the furniture on the day before the sale and of her bidding for items at the sale. Actually, some quite nice pieces of furniture were purchased and at a very good price: settees, tables, chairs, wardrobes, chests of drawers etc. were all obtained in this manner.

Our social life was of course limited but not entirely non-existent. There was no television or for that matter radio as far as we were concerned during this period, so entertainment was made by ourselves and consisted in the main of playing card games either among ourselves or when we invited our friends, or visited them. Many a good evening was spent in this way. My own outside interests included several organizations. I joined the Boy Cubs and progressed through to Scouting, spending many happy times away camping. I was quite a keen member and obtained a number of badges for various activities. I attended Sunday school regularly at 3pm each Sunday. I was at the Congregational Church in my early youth and can remember being presented with a certificate for 48 attendances out of 52. I think perhaps the Congregational Church was nearest to us - about one mile and I think perhaps my parents were glad of a couple of hours peace on a Sunday afternoon. Later I joined the choir at St. John's Church. This was strictly Church of England. I cannot say that I ever had a singing voice but I was accepted and received 6d per week for attending choir practice of an evening mid-week and the evening service on Sunday. I must have looked the picture of innocence in my black surplice with white frilly collar.

I seemed to have a great interest in bands, particularly those of a military nature. The Boys Brigade from, I think, London camped annually in a field opposite our home. I always took great interest in them and felt a thrill as they marched down past our house with drums beating and bugles blowing. On one occasion, I think a Sunday, the Salvation Army came marching down our road led by a great band, drummers, big base-drum, bugles, cornets etc. I am not aware of my age at the time but probably no more than six. I could not resist falling in behind them and marching with the band. We seemed to march for miles and miles and finished up in a large field at North Bersted little more than a mile from my home around 8pm. I can only remember thereafter, that my father arrived on his bike, extremely agitated and took me back home where I was well and truly chastised. It seems that when my parents discovered I was missing they searched everywhere for me, not thinking that I might have "followed the band". My absence obviously caused them alarm.

At one stage my parents produced a piano which presumably they hoped I would begin to play. My mother had an ear for music and although she was unable to read music, could play all the modern tunes by ear. Alas I was not at all musical. I had weekly lessons over a very long period and even attended theory lessons every Saturday morning, but it was not to be. I did not enjoy it and made little progress until, in the end, I had to admit defeat.

I always had a great interest in sports but was not particularly brilliant at anything. I could sprint very well and often won races at the school sports, the 100yds being my best. Rugby was not played in this part of the country; hockey was a game for girl's. Tennis was unavailable, which left football - the ordinary man's sport. I first commenced to play this in the school playground at playtime and dinner breaks. The playground was hard asphalt and we played with a tennis ball, the goal posts being chalked on the school wall. I volunteered to be the goalkeeper, perhaps because my Uncle Bert - a giant of a man, kept goal for Bognor Town F.C. or more likely because no one else would take on this unpleasant job. I fairly soon made a name for myself however by diving at full length for the ball on the hard playground. Goodness knows to what state my clothes became but I know both knees and elbows were quite badly grazed. However, I had made my mark and soon found that whenever it was a case of selection, I was picked, and later on, picked to play in goal for the school in their official matches against other schools on properly marked grass football pitches with real goal posts and nets. I must have done reasonably well because I progressed to playing for my town's boys team and then almost the ultimate: my county of Sussex. For this I was awarded my county colours and became something of a celebrity. Boys from Bognor had never before been included in the county team, yet here was I and another young boy from North Bersted school (Billy Reid) playing for Sussex. It was a peculiar feeling to be out and about in the town being pointed out as "that young fellow who plays football for Sussex." I would like to have gone further and played for my country, but when my name came up I was over 14 and not eligible.

As soon as I was old enough, I found myself a holiday job as errand boy to earn some money. My first job was probably at the age of 9 or 10, delivering papers before attending school. I remember working for Smith's at the railway station in Bognor. We would arrive about 6:30am, unload the papers from the train when it arrived, take them to the book stall for sorting and each collect our own round in a large newspaper sack. I would set off on my round to the south of Bognor and deliver, subsequently going home for breakfast before starting school. I think I had a bicycle at this time for getting to and fro although the paper round had to be done on foot. I later took other jobs which entailed working on Saturdays and some of them after school at 4pm also. I doubt whether there were many retail outlets I did not try - grocers, green-grocers, bread/cake shops, milkmen, and butchers. I always gave fish-shops a miss as I was not particularly fond of the smell and messiness of wet fish. However the pocket money that I earned, small though it was, was very useful. The work in some cases involved full time during school holidays. I remember when I worked in the bakery of Leslie's Cafe at Bognor. It was an early start to bake the bread around 6am. I went there before school started, but on a Saturday we finished about 3pm, and I was paid something like 5 shillings (25p) for 6am to 8-30am Monday to Friday and 6am to 3pm on Saturday. Often, though not every week, I would call at the dairy on my way home Saturdays after payment and buy for my Mother two ounces of best cream butter. A treat perhaps for her and something I felt she needed.

Family holidays were really non-existent. My father would have two weeks off from his work during the year but there was no money to go away on holiday. Instead they would have days out, perhaps a day at Brighton or another at Portsmouth or Southsea, Littlehampton or Worthing: never very far. We went by train and spent the day looking around, going to a cafe for lunch. Never very exciting, but a change. On one occasion travelling back by train I sat by the door in a single compartment and played around with the door catch. In those days carriage doors were opened from the inside by a latch. Needless to say, the door flew open while the train was travelling at some speed. My father grabbed hold of me and held me in, but was unable to get the carriage door closed until the train slowed down - another chastisement for me of course but one that was well deserved.

At school, I was not the brightest of pupils, rather the reverse, but managed to hold my own with the remainder of the class. It was a boys-only school, the girls being separated and taught in another building. I had a great interest in figures and arithmetic, probably because my tables had been drummed into me at the age of five. This was to stand me in good stead later in life. The possibility of moving on from an elementary education to a grammar school education was almost non-existent and as to getting to a university in order to gain a degree, this was quite out of the question. Only those who could afford to pay went to the grammar school and likewise for university education. There was one tiny glimmer of hope: that was for boys of eleven to take the scholarship examination, from which three boys only were selected from ALL schools in the area. The lucky three were given a place either at Chichester Secondary School or Midhurst Grammar. I took the examination but, of course, did not come near the top three places. I well remember one question of that examination. "If it takes four minutes to boil an egg, how long will it take to boil six eggs?" The obvious answer was four minutes if they are all boiled together but this was too obvious for me. I just thought no way could such an answer be required and gave it as 24 minutes - of course I was wrong. There were no school leaving examinations or certificates or qualifications and so I just left school at the age of fourteen with a moderate report and basically qualified for nothing.

There is no doubt that this period of my early life shaped my thinking and views which destined the remainder of my life. The poverty, lack of money, fear of unemployment and fear of destitution in old age clearly caused me, if not consciously, to think about the future. Lack of an adequate money supply has been a great fear of mine always. Hence, even when there is sufficient and more I have been unable to spend easily except for necessities. I often wonder why I was so keen to enter the Royal Navy. It could not have been because my next door neighbour was a stoker petty officer I am sure, although this could have tipped the balance of which of the three services I might join, if that was to be my future. Certainly the services offered permanent employment with a pension at the end after 22 years. At the same time food, clothing and shelter were provided and there was plenty of opportunity for promotion bringing greater pay and pension for those with ambition - and I was certainly one of those. I could not go into the Air Force because at that time they only took boys from grammar schools. This therefore left me with the Army or Navy to choose from. The Army held little attraction for me and, perhaps clouded by my next door neighbour's apparently exotic life, decided I would try the Navy, but if possible to enter a higher grade than just a seaman and that my ultimate ambition would be to reach the exulted rank of Chief Petty Officer by 22 years.

I cannot answer for how my political views were formed. One would think from the foregoing that they would be very strongly socialist but this was not so, quite the reverse, they were and always have been Conservative. I never felt, and perhaps should have done so, "why should some have so much and others so little". There was, as far as I can remember, no particular view or pressures one way or the other from my parents. I always felt that however poor one was, by hard work and integrity one could be lifted from the rut, although this was not the case with my father. I also thought that everyone's destiny was their own and should not be controlled by the state. If there was wealth among a certain proportion of the people, provided it was used for the benefit of the country then all must prosper, so why envy them? England was a great and powerful country. The British Empire took charge of the whole world and no one dared challenge us: a country and an empire of which one and all were proud and honoured to belong.

ENTRY TO THE ROYAL NAVY

On leaving school at the age of fourteen my mind was firmly made up as to my future - it was of course to join the Royal Navy. This, however, could not be until I was fifteen and so I took a job as errand boy to a shoe shop in York Road, Bognor Regis. The job entailed not only delivering boots and shoes that had been purchased from the shop, but cleaning the large shop windows and keeping the pavement in front of the shop clean. A general "dog's body". making tea etc. and sometimes loaned to the fur shop next door to make their fur deliveries.

It was for me just a stop gap job while I investigated and attempted to enter the Navy at a higher level. I felt that it would be nice to enter as an Artificer of which there were three types: engine room, electrical or ordnance (guns) and would mean virtually starting as a petty officer. Electrical Artificer appealed to me, but I knew I was up against it - all such entries having come from Grammar Schools and I having not had that kind of education. My parents paid for me to have private tuition at home a couple of times a week and one of my ex-teachers came along to coach me. I would have to sit the Artificer Apprentices Examination, held twice yearly and sent off for the appropriate papers. I worked very hard and sat the first examination in Portsmouth in 1933. Of course I failed but not downhearted started preparations for the next examinations with some experience behind me now. At the next examination, I passed but was much too far down the list to be selected. I think I came 733rd but they only required the first 30. I had to abandon this idea at this stage as I would have been too old by the time of the next examination.

My only recourse now was to enter at a lower grade and I decided I would like wireless telegraphy. My enquiries elicited the fact that it was not possible to join direct into the wireless telegraphy branch but that it was necessary to first join as a boy seaman and then at a later date to be selected for the communications branch. I was by now right down to the bottom, but still determined and so off I went to Portsmouth early in 1934 to see the recruiting officer. "How long do you want to join for son" he said to me. "Twenty two years" said I. "Well" he said "you'd better try twelve years first and see if you like it." The alternative to this was seven years, followed by five on the reserve - of no interest to me at all - so I settled for twelve years from the age of eighteen. The entry examination caused me no problems at all but the strict medical examination was not at all plain sailing. A doctor decided I had varicocele, a small lump in the groin, probably a vein, which had to be removed before I could be accepted. Undaunted I returned home and arranged though my doctor for the operation to be performed at the local Bognor Cottage Hospital. I think the operation was early in May and by June I was back again to Portsmouth for a further medical - this time successful. I was told to return home and await call up, which duly came in July.

I was to report to H.M.S. St. Vincent, a shore establishment for the training of boys, on July 9th 1934. A railway warrant to Gosport was included with papers and brief instructions of what I should or should not bring. Duly on the appointed day, I set off, without as far as I can remember any farewells but, looking back, my heart must have been heavy.

At H.M.S. St. Vincent, I joined approximately thirty other boys, some tearful, some not. We were fairly smartly relieved of our civilian clothing, everything including socks, underpants etc. and kitted out with naval clothing, mostly two of everything:

- boots
- navy blue socks
- flannel vests
- white duck suits (rough white drill)
- blue "going ashore" suit
- cap with box ribbon
- two flannel vests marked NS (nightshirt)
- a wooden type with our name printed
- a bundle of clothes stops (cord to tie washing to the line)
- a housewife (small linen roll up, with cotton, needles, wool etc.)

We were then split into various houses, introduced to our instructors (petty officers) and the instructor boys. The latter were senior boys who had completed their training but had been retained to help with new recruits. They were boys with an aggressive manner. Subsequently we were taken to our dormitory to be allocated a bed. This was followed by a shower – all boys together in the one shower room, much to the dismay of the most modest. Finally, we had an evening meal, a lecture on establishment rules and regulations, then to bed.

The first six months were to be spent in the new-entry block as seaman boys second class. This breaking in period was fairly tough I suppose but necessarily so in view of what we would have to face in the future. Reveille was at 6am by bugle with the instructor boy chasing around the beds to ensure everyone was out by 6:01 - if they weren't, they would be tipped out. On with boots, socks and duck trousers only. Dash to the bathroom for

Boys of H.M.S. St. Vincent 1935. WPE front row right

wash and clean teeth and back to fall in fully dressed by 6:15 when a cup of thick cocoa and one ships biscuit (hard and tasteless) was issued. At 6:30 it was fall in again - always in the open air, and time for drills: marching, physical training or over the mast until 8am when we had three quarters of an hour for breakfast and preparation for the day ahead. The mast drill, which I think happened every day, entailed climbing the rigging up the Jacob's Ladder and over the mast at the top - about 150ft (50m) high, down the other side and fall in. Last one down caught the tail end of the rope carried by instructor boys, especially for whacking out at new entries. Incidentally, the mast was fitted with a safety net at the bottom. At 8:45 it was fall in again fully and properly dressed, to be inspected by our instructors and then marched to prayers on the parade ground, followed by morning divisions at 9am when the whole establishment were fallen in and inspected by the divisional officers, reporting to the commodore. Following this ritual, divisions were dispersed to their various commitments which was normally half the day at school to complete, or further one's education and half the day on professional training. As far as new entries were concerned, the first week was spent sewing our names into every item of clothing. Our type stamped the name on the garment in black or white dye, then the name was sewn in, by what I think was called stocking stitch. On socks, handkerchiefs and other small items the name was stamped on tape, sewn in and the tape stitched to the garment We even had to go over the "N.S." on our nightshirts in navy blue wool.

I cannot recall any particular difficulties during this training period other than, at first, I had great difficulty in marching. I tried so very hard, that my right arm would insist on going forward with my right leg and likewise with my left leg. I was in much trouble for this - had I only been relaxed and let my arms swing naturally all would have been well. It took me a few weeks to learn. My other problem was with swimming. Although I had lived by the sea all my life, I had never learnt to swim. Most of the other boys could swim well but in any event it is necessary to pass the test of swimming two lengths of the bath fully clothed in a duck suit before passing out of the new entry section. The method of training was to make boys jump into the deep water and a physical training instructor stood at the side with a long pole. Far be it that this pole was used for rescues - it was used to push boys away from the edge until they had to swim to keep afloat and once one reached the side they would immediately be pushed back again. I learnt to swim but never by orthodox swimming strokes which I am unable to do to this day. I was able to pass the swimming test in January 1935.

Not all boys took to this period of training although most did. I remember one friend - his name was Greenwood and his father a Naval Warrant Officer living in Southsea. He could not accept the training and had to leave after about six weeks. He was a non-swimmer also but was given an honourable discharge. We were not allowed any shore leave during this period although our parents could visit on Sunday afternoons if they wished. I do not remember my own parents visiting the establishment. They would have had difficulty with the train fare and my father's shift work was not exactly conducive to a day out like that. However, it did happen that summer leave of two weeks fell during my training period so I was able to be at home for two weeks during August.

The pay of a second class boy was 5s 3d (26p) per week although we were not given this amount. Pay-day was on Wednesday and we received one shilling (5p) which we could spend in the canteen where various sweets etc. could be bought. Pay-day was quite a ritual. The whole establishment mustered and fell in as for divisions on the bugle call at 11am. After being checked that no one was absent, divisions in turn were marched to the paymaster at the pay table. When your name was called you stepped smartly up to the table, saluted, shouted your ships company number - mine was 5025 at St. Vincent - removed cap with the right hand and held it, flat top uppermost in front of the paymaster. When he had placed the due amount on the cap, the left hand had to come across smartly to cover it, left turn and march away, subsequently to pocket the money and replace cap.

At the end of the first three months came the passing out exams, before which we had to declare our interest in becoming wireless telegraphy, signalman or seaman. I opted for W.T. of course. I came third of the thirty boys in the school exam and passed out practically, in seamanship and swimming. Lo and behold, when the allocation of places was made, I was nominated for a signalman. I was not only disappointed but furious and officially requested to see my divisional officer on the matter. He told me that the top two boys wanted to be telegraphists and several beneath me, but they could not put all the best boys into the telegraphy branch. They wanted some of the brighter ones in signals as well. His answer neither convinced me nor suited me. The following Monday when we reformed in our new divisions out of the new entry block, I made strong representations to the divisional Petty Officer and thence to the School Master, to the effect that I was just not interested in becoming a signalman. I was told to carry on as normal but within forty-eight hours came the message that I was to be transferred to wireless telegraphy and did so forthwith - my first battle won!

On passing out of the new entry division we were made first class boys with a rise in pay from 5s 3d to 7s 6d (37.5p) of which we received 1s 6d (7.5p) weekly. We were also given a name ribbon to tie with a bow on our caps instead of the box pleat worn previously and allowed half a day's shore leave weekly either on Wednesday or Sunday from 1pm to 6pm. The rigorous 6am call was dropped in favour of a 7am reveille and breakfast at 8am. Of my 1s 6d I was able to buy some margarine to go with my biscuit and cocoa at 7am which I kept in my ditty box (a box issued for keeping personal papers and letters etc.) Altogether, life was very much more pleasant.

We still continued with a half day of normal schooling and a half day learning our professional duties: Morse code, procedures, technical on Naval wireless sets etc. and learning something of a signalman's duties such as semaphore, flashing lamps, heliograph and flag signals. We had two weeks leave at Easter, two in the summer and two at Christmas, plus plenty of sport either in evenings or on Saturdays. I played football for the establishment and took part in another rigorous sport known as "field gun". I was in the divisional team for this. It consisted of the team running about 100 yards (100 m) with the field gun on ropes, dismantling the gun to get it over a barrier, reassembling, running another 100 yards with it, stop, set it up and fire three rounds. It was great fun which I thoroughly enjoyed. Additionally, there was plenty of physical training: swimming, running and all the other keep fit activities.

The training continued until October 1935 with various intermediate examinations on the way. October was to be the finals. In these I came top at school and won the class prize which was a crocodile leather writing case. I also came top of technical for which I won the class prize of a leather zip up toilet case. Both of these prizes I still treasure. I felt quite confident and pleased with my efforts and now eager to get to sea and put into practice all that I had learnt.

Competing in Field Gun event

Additionally, I had won two field gun medals for twice being in the winning team out of three competitions. I was sure that I had made the right choice. On reflection, had I passed the artificers examination and entered by that method I might well have been up against boys who had been given a better start than myself and may have been forever struggling. Certainly I would have been at some disadvantage, whereas, by being a telegraphist I had everything before me.

TO SEA

After two week's home leave, I returned to H.M.S. St. Vincent to await draft, during which time schooling and training continued. This lasted for a very short period as on 17th October I was drafted to H.M.S. Iron Duke at Portsmouth. I had been allotted to the Portsmouth division because my home was nearer Portsmouth than either of the other two Divisions: one at Chatham and one at Devonport. At this stage, all boys who had passed out and been awarded their telegraphist wings were each allocated to the depot nearest their home. So became the first parting of the ways. I left St. Vincent with a character "Very Good" and efficiency of "Superior".

H.M.S. Iron Duke was a battleship which had given excellent service during the First World War but by now (1935) was somewhat outdated and belonged to what was known as the Reserve Fleet. This meant that she pottered around home shores more or less as a training ship but ready to be put into immediate service in the event of hostilities. My draft there was to accustom me to shipboard life, combined with continuous training and schooling. I was issued with a hammock, mattress and blankets and had to learn how to sling a hammock and more importantly how to get in and out of it, without falling flat on the mess tables. Hammocks were of course slung on iron rails fitted to the deck head over the mess tables. It was also necessary to learn how to lash a hammock on rising each morning. It was lashed by seven half hitches into a sausage like shape and securely tied with the owner's name facing outwards and then stowed in the hammock locker until required the following night. They were inspected before stowage and woe betide any boy who had not lashed his hammock correctly. Washing was somewhat primitive - in tin bowls in a wash / shower room. We learnt to be cooks of the mess according to a rota. This meant collecting the food for each meal from the ship's galley and dividing it into portions according to the number in the mess. It also meant what was known as dishing up (washing up). For this a large steel utensil with a handle was used to obtain hot water from the wash room and the dishes were washed with hard yellow soap and dried by cloth. It was all most interesting and to me quite enjoyable. We were split into watches for leave, but boys had to be back on board by 7pm, so it was only worth going ashore on Saturday or Sunday when shore leave commenced at 1pm. On other days shore leave was granted from 4pm.

I joined H.M.S. Iron Duke at Spithead on the 17th October two days after my seventeenth birthday. The Home Fleet was assembling at Spithead in preparation for King George V's jubilee review - the 25th year of his reign. The number of ships at anchor in the Solent was phenomenal: they stretched from Portsmouth right through to the Needles in about eight lines. Far more warships than I was ever likely to see again - far more than the U.S. Navy plus the Royal Navy together at the present time. There were battleships, battle-cruisers, cruisers, destroyers, aircraft-carriers, minesweepers, tugs and warships of every description. Iron Duke, being of the Reserve Fleet was anchored well out towards the end of the line of capital ships. The review took place on the 21st October - Trafalgar Day, when all ships were dressed overall with flags from stem to stem, every ship having the same flags in the same sequence and all being broken (raised) together with morning colours at 8am - a tremendous sight to witness. At 11am, after each ship had been thoroughly scrubbed and cleaned, all brass work highly polished, sailors and officers dressed in their "number one" suits

Spithead Review 1935

and were fallen in on deck, to line the ships side from stem to stern. The King and Queen Mary sailed from Portsmouth in the Royal Yacht: "Victoria and Albert", also dressed overall and her sides manned by her crew, all in blue jumpers white trousers and white plimsolls. They sailed through each line of ships commencing with the Commander in Chief Home Fleet in H.M.S. Nelson. As the Victoria and Albert passed each ship, the Captain called for three cheers which were given in unison, hats being raised. Celebrations continued all day, with the undressing of ships all together at sunset followed by a magnificent fireworks display and officer's parties in the wardrooms of various ships.

This was all a rather exciting start to my life at sea but by the 22nd October it was all over and routine back to normal. The problem was the orderly dispersal of so many ships from Spithead and to get well clear of the area, Iron Duke was sent to Torbay, just off Torquay, where we anchored whilst awaiting dispersal of the fleet, eventually returning to Portsmouth where we anchored at Spithead until the 29th October. Then it was off again to Torquay, Plymouth, back to Torquay and thence Portland at anchor on the 7th November.

This short period was an introduction to shipboard life and I realised that Iron Duke was just a transit ship for me whilst I awaited draft to my first ship as part of the complement. This came in no uncertain fashion during the mini-cruise to Plymouth. I was to join H.M.S. Nelson, flagship of the Home Fleet – a very large and diversified fleet under the command of Admiral Sir Roger Backhouse. How very proud I was and how excited to transfer my kit bag and hammock to the launch at Portland to be transferred to this magnificent ship...the pride of the Royal Navy.

H.M.S. NELSON

H.M.S. Nelson remained at Portland until early December 1935, going to sea for three or four days each week on exercises with other ships of the Home Fleet which were also stationed at Portland. These were minor exercises in formations, station keeping, torpedo attacks and minor gunnery exercises. In December, the ships returned to their home ports for Christmas leave of two weeks, taken in two parts: either 15th December to 29th or 29th to 12th January. On the 13th January, 1936 the annual Spring Cruise began which culminated in meeting the Mediterranean Fleet off Gibraltar where major war exercises took place between what was known as the Red and Blue Fleets. Our first call was to be to Villagarcia in Arosa Bay, Northern Spain. This was a five day voyage across the Bay of Biscay, during which exercises were carried out the whole time. The ship took on a war footing with the company in three watches (instead of the peacetime four) and communications were at their peak. We had to maintain communications with the Battle Cruiser Squadron, each Cruiser Squadron and each Destroyer Flotilla leader as well as the other Battleships of our line. Additionally, being the Commander in Chief's Flagship, we had a constant link with the Admiralty.

WPE on H.M.S. Nelson

Further communications tasks were the interception of Foreign Transmissions (I.F.T.) which meant hours of scanning all frequencies to read messages from foreign warships, usually in code, which were sent off to the Admiralty for deciphering -- unfortunately we never heard the results of this effort, but it would have been more than interesting! We also had to keep watch on commercial channels for merchant shipping which could be in distress.

The journey across the Bay of Biscay was not particularly to my liking. At the best of times there is an Atlantic Swell across the bay and at others it can be very rough. Big as Nelson was, she was prone to rolling. The triple sixteen inch turrets on the foredeck and high superstructure made her somewhat top heavy, added to that, the very long bow gave her a twisting motion to add to the roll, so it was similar to a corkscrew motion. Needless to say I was seasick, felt terrible and was interested in nothing except getting back to harbour. It seemed terrible to be seasick in a ship of this size, but I was not alone. The only relief, as I found on many occasions subsequently, was to get into a hammock, which although appeared to be moving and swinging, was in fact staying almost still whilst the ship rolled around it. Of course, hammocks would only be slung between 8pm and 7am, but at least there was some relief at night. What a relief it was to anchor in Arosa Bay on 17th January. For the first time I began to wonder if I had done right by joining the Navy, but it was such a relief to be at anchor - and still - that the nightmare of the last three days was soon forgotten.

I remember little of Villagarcia; it was just a small fishing port in Northern Spain, with a tiny town, but it was my first visit to a foreign port. I found the Spaniards there to be a poor, but friendly people although none could speak English. They bartered with us for small gifts that we would take home as souvenirs, but it was certainly not a place to "live it up". We sailed on 22nd January for a two day trip to Gibraltar which was quite uneventful and pleasant, and I might say lovely to be in a warmer climate after England. During the night of 21st January King George V passed away, not unexpectedly, as he had been ill for some while. Apart from flying the Union Jack at half-mast there was little we could do and there would be no question of the Fleet returning for the State Funeral. The Prince of Wales, Edward was proclaimed King Edward VIII and life had to continue as normal.

We remained at Gibraltar for two weeks, as always, going to sea during the week to carry out exercises. The main exercises or conflict with the Mediterranean Fleet was to take place in the latter half of February and early March. It would have to be on a restricted scale this year because a large part of the Mediterranean Fleet was tied up in the Eastern Mediterranean where Italy, under Mussolini, was preparing to invade and take over Ethiopia. As far as we were concerned of course, a vital link in our communications to the middle and Far East was threatened - the Suez Canal.

During early February we had a short break by a visit to Las Palmas (Canary Islands) which we visited from 10th to 14th. A most pleasant change and a lovely island with a perfect climate long before the days of the tourist. Here too the people were friendly and some could speak a little broken English, but enough to get them by and sell to us their souvenirs. I suppose we were friendly to them but they, like many foreigners at the time, were frightened to death of the great British Navy. The remainder of this extended cruise was spent back at Gibraltar from 17th February to 14th May, constantly exercising with and against ships of the Mediterranean Fleet, the largest and most efficient Fleet in the world. Gibraltar was quite a good port at which to be based. It was somewhat confined, only being a rock, but a rock which was interesting to climb, with rock monkeys to discover and watch. There was just one main shopping street through the centre absolutely full of souvenir shops and bars. All spoke English, there was nightlife aplenty and everything was remarkably cheap as well as being unique and unusual to our own country. The climate was excellent, warm and sunny for most of the time, so much so that one afternoon I lay on the harbour wall and fell asleep just dressed in my shorts and no shirt. I awoke with a somewhat red tummy and shoulders and by the evening was one huge blister from my neck to my waist. I could not possibly don a shirt and so had to report to sick bay where I was retained and treated. Worst perhaps, was the anger of the doctor when he saw me. I was called all the names possible, the politest of which was "stupid idiot" and informed that I would be put on the Commander's charge for wilfully incapacitating myself for duty. I was of course scared stiff as this would have meant perhaps 14 days jankers. This was a punishment, involving getting up one hour before all others and scrubbing decks, having all meal breaks curtailed and falling in during the evening where one was made to run round in a circle for an hour, holding an iron bar above the head. I never received this punishment but learned very quickly to have an answer ready when things had gone wrong. I remonstrated with the doctor over my sunburn and told him I would not do such a thing for pleasure or any other purpose and had accidentally fallen asleep. After three days when I was ready for discharge to normal duties, he told me he thought I had been punished enough and that he would take no further action. He was right, I had learned my lesson.

On 14th May we left Gibraltar for a four day, uneventful trip straight back to Portsmouth with a calm crossing of the Bay of Biscay. The return was made to give the ship's company delayed Easter leave of two weeks, given in two parts, that is two weeks to each watch. On 29th June it was time to leave again for a return to Gibraltar and the Mediterranean where the Ethiopia/Abyssinian trouble with Italy was continuing. However, this was short lived and in Mid-July H.M.S. Nelson returned to her home port at Portsmouth for summer leave and the annual Navy Week at Portsmouth followed by preparation for the Autumn Cruise and exercises.

Navy Week was an annual event for the Royal Navy when all warships of the Home Fleet returned to their home ports in order to give the public the opportunity of visiting their warships. The event always took place from the first Saturday in August for a whole week and Portsmouth was the largest. The dockyard was simply a mass of people from noon each day until 6pm, with so many ships to see, including Nelson's flagship -- H.M.S. Victory. There were numerous events taking place throughout the dockyard and the whole thing was a wonderful day out for people but far too much to be seen in one day. Ships, particularly the larger ones, had to be rigorously cordoned off into those parts that visitors could visit and those that they could not, but it was all a lot of fun.

My times of leave were spent at my home in Bognor Regis where, for some unknown reason, I was treated quite royally. There was little to do at Bognor although it was very pleasant in the summer months. As a seaside resort, it was full of visitors and they appeared to be quite glamorous times. Certainly a sailor's uniform was an attraction to the opposite sex, although until this time I had little interest in girls. I did meet and become interested in a girl of about my own age, her name was Doreen, who came from Mexborough in Yorkshire and was in service to a man and his wife, of middle class, from Bognor. I suppose the association lasted about six months, during which time she persuaded me to visit her home with her during her holiday. I was not at all impressed with Mexborough or Yorkshire. It was a coal-mining town, in fact her father was a coal miner. The whole place was dirty, dilapidated, and depressing; the people lived in poverty. If I had ever thought I was poor - and I can never remember thinking such - then I was wealthy compared with this. It may be that my disillusionment was such as to bring an end to this association. I met a number of other girls, but none that interested me sufficiently for more than one or two dates. Recreation was found in the form of cinema films, roller skating, dancing - at which I have never been a success and often to watch England's Test Cricket. There was of course no television in those days, so in the local pavilion grounds was erected a large green board painted like a cricket field. On this board were symbols indicating men and one could watch the bowler coming up to bowl and the batsman hit the ball. It was controlled by men behind the screen, connected to the test match by telephone and showing the imaginary moves of the activity. It looked realistic enough and was a pleasant way to spend a sunny, warm day, sitting in a deck chair. England's cricket was at its height at this time, the greatest adversary being Australia.

On 8th September, H.M.S. Nelson left Portsmouth for the Autumn Cruise which was to be in Scotland, with the Home Fleet assembling at Greenock. From here we operated on exercises until 15th, then on to Loch Ewe, Scapa Flow, Invergordon, down to the other side of Scotland, Rosyth and finally back down South to Portland. Exercises were in progress the whole time, but nevertheless, time was available in ports to visit places of interest and I had my first calls to Glasgow, Kirkwall, and Edinburgh. During this cruise I had reached the important age of 18 which meant that my boy service came to an end and I started on my real and accountable career of the 12 years' service for which I had signed up. I moved from the boys mess to the communications mess, among the men, and was put on to full watch keeping duties. These were forenoon (8am to noon) and first (8pm to midnight) on one day, afternoon (12 to 4pm) and Middle (midnight to 4am) the next, followed by First Dog (4pm to 6pm) and Morning (4am to 8am) and on the fourth day Last Dog (6pm - 8pm.) My assessment on completion of boy service and up to the age of 18 was: "character: very good, efficiency: superior". Thereafter we would be assessed annually on 31st December and every assessment until my promotion to commissioned rank was the same except for my first assessment for leading Telegraphist and Petty Officer Telegraphist which according to the rules could not be higher than Satisfactory as far as efficiency was concerned.

On 9th November 1936 whilst at Portland, I passed the examination for advancement to full telegraphist and was duly upgraded in January 1937 before the commencement of the Spring Cruise. We finally returned to Portsmouth in mid-November for a break and Christmas leave.

As in previous years the ship sailed again in January 1937 for annual exercises with the Mediterranean Fleet. This year the political scene had changed somewhat. Although the Abyssinian crisis had been resolved, Spain had thrown out its Royal Family and declared itself independent under General Franco -- virtually a dictatorship. Hitler was active in Germany, occupying the Rhineland and at home, King Edward abdicated the throne on December 11th 1936 and his brother George was declared King George VI. Whilst we could do little about the internal affairs of Spain, they were laying claim to Gibraltar situated at their southern tip and we had our shipping to protect. A heavy naval presence at and around the entrance to the Mediterranean was therefore desirable. During the period from January to the end of March we visited Valencia, Palma, Barcelona, and Tangiers. The fleet exercises took place as usual to demonstrate a show of strength. Certainly the firing of a broadside of Nelson's nine, 16" guns was enough to frighten anyone, including all of us on board. When these nine guns fired together, the ship literally lifted out of the water on the recoil. Anything moveable was knocked down, all wooden doors and furniture had to be removed before firing, or they would be smashed. This Spring Cruise ended back in Portsmouth in time for Easter leave after which thoughts had to be turned to the Coronation ceremony of King George VI which was to be on May 13th.

My last cruise in Nelson as part of her ship's company began on 27th April, although at that time I was not to know that it would be my last. We spent nine days at Portland before dispersing for our Coronation ports. Each ship or groups of smaller ships were assigned to ports all around the country and Nelson was to go to Southend, my place of birth. We were there from 7th May to 13th and what a wonderful time it was. Officers and crew were feted wherever they went and people could not do enough for us; it was like one wonderful party, with the ship open to visitors over the weekend. Coronation day itself was just a wonderful day, the ship dressed overall of course and great celebrations. After sunset, fireworks, etc. we had to return to Spithead overnight in preparation for the King's review of the Fleet. As for the jubilee review for King George V, all ships of the home Fleet assembled at Spithead for this great occasion. Once more, the Solent was full to overflowing with the mass of ships of every conceivable type. This was all a repeat of what I had witnessed from Iron Duke less than two years before, but this time in even greater splendour as I was witnessing it all from the most important ship in the review, the flagship of Commander in Chief of the Fleet. After the review, as before, ships dispersed and Nelson, with others of the Home Fleet went to Portland for four weeks of the endless exercises, finishing this period with a visit to Guernsey for 10 days of relaxation and enjoyment. It certainly was, in the most glorious weather and with great hospitality from the Channel Islanders. As usual on these courtesy visits, the ship was open to visitors at weekends of which the local population took full advantage, but then Nelson was a ship really worth visiting. On 28th June Nelson returned to Portsmouth for summer leave and the Annual Navy Week in Portsmouth, whilst I found that I was to be transferred to R.N. Barracks Portsmouth. The particular reason for the transfer I knew not, other than perhaps to give some other youngster the opportunity of going to sea.

H.M.S MAIDSTONE

The signal school to which I was drafted was a separate section of the Royal Naval Barracks and apart from the weekly divisions every Friday for the whole barracks, ran its own affairs. The weekly divisions, was a ritual, whereby every division of the barracks paraded in their best suits, officers with swords and medals. They were inspected first by the Divisional Officer and finally by the Commodore of the barracks. This was followed by a march past in long lines abreast with the emphasis on keeping those lines absolutely straight whilst marching and at "eyes-left" or "eyes-right" whilst passing the podium containing the dignitaries.

I was appointed as personal messenger to the four expert Signal Officers who controlled communications of the Royal Navy. W1, a Lieutenant Commander Walmsley, was in general charge. W2, a Lieutenant Williams was in charge of technical matters. W3, the Hon. DC Cairns, whom I was to serve with again later in charge of organization and W4 a Lieutenant Dickie Courage who went far later. These gentlemen all shared one office and I sat outside at a small desk, at the ready to run messages for them. I did the job to their satisfaction, but generally found it rather boring, although I got along well with my four masters.

During this period there were distinct rumblings of unrest throughout Europe. Italy was giving aid, by means of volunteers, to the insurgents in Spain. Hitler was in the process of annexing Austria and Czechoslovakia. The British Prime Minister, Chamberlain was seeking appeasement with Hitler and Mussolini. The British Foreign Minister Anthony Eden resigned in protest against this action. At the same time Japan invaded China in the Far East and was making progress having captured Nanking. My draft to the signal school in R.N. Barracks could not therefore last for long and on 10th February 1938 I was sent to H.M.S. Dunedin of the reserve fleet.

I can remember little of the time I spent in Dunedin, which in any event lasted little more than two months until 25th April when I was sent to join H.M.S. Maidstone being built at Glasgow. H.M.S. Maidstone was the latest Submarine Depot ship and destined to join the Mediterranean fleet as soon as possible. She had been built with every modem convenience, to service and supply submarines, and to give their crews comfortable accommodation when they returned from patrol. She was a very high sided ship, not of great speed or manoeuvrability, but purely as a moveable base for submarines and a communications centre. I was proud to be a telegraphist, as fully part of the complement of this ship fitted with all the latest and up to date wireless equipment and even more thrilled to know we were going to join the elite – the Mediterranean fleet.

We commissioned with a full complement on the 4th May and sailed for Portsmouth on the 5th where we spent six weeks working up, that is, testing and familiarizing ourselves with all the equipment as well as becoming proficient in its operation. Finally on the 14th June we bade farewell to Portsmouth and set course for the Mediterranean. I remember well this first trip because although it was not rough, there was the usual swell in the Bay of Biscay and I had two days of quite bad seasickness. Maidstone was after all, a high sided vessel, with the wireless offices on the bridge and had a great tendency to roll with the swell. Seasickness was not a reason for failing to carry out normal duties and therefore one continued the watch accompanied by a bucket. Not easy to read Morse code and be sick at the same time. Our first stop was Tangiers in North Africa for two days, then across to what was by now a familiar place to me, Gibraltar for one day and on to Malta which we reached on 24th June. During this period, on 30th May, I sat and passed the examination for Trained Operator – this would give me one star above my Telegraphist wings as well an increase in pay but more importantly give me some status.

Malta, of which I was to see much in the coming months and years, was a fascinating place, untouched by tourists at this time. It was first and foremost a naval port and island as well as the home base for the tremendous Mediterranean Fleet, far larger than the home base for the Home Fleet and quite the epitome of efficiency. Its narrow, cobbled streets simply thronged with sailors. Straight Street, known to sailors as "the Gut" was a long straight street, quite narrow and full of bars on either side, nothing else. Outside of each was the Maltese proprietor persuading the sailors to enter his bar and amongst all this were the numerous houses of ill repute. It was just one long sight of sailors in various stages of drunkenness. There were many sights to be seen on the island, normally by ghari -- a horse drawn cab, after a good deal of haggling with the driver. There was a signal school and a gunnery school at Ghain Tuffieha. Swimming was excellent in any of the many bays. A truly wonderful island to visit and stay.

Our first visit was very brief, just three days, enough for the Captain to make his calls on the Flag Officer, Malta and Commander in Chief, Mediterranean Fleet among others. Then we were off on a cruise up the Adriatic to Yugoslavia, in order to show the British flag. We went to Tivat for six days, on to Kolior for four days and Crikvenica for ten days before returning to Malta on 28th August. This was an excellent cruise in the most glorious weather. Whilst at sea, the ship stopped both morning and evenings for half an hour to allow swimming over the side, this was usually wonderful in the warm, salty, tideless waters of the Mediterranean. I had by this time involved myself in the ship's football team and we played a local team at each of the visits. Every one of the small towns was of considerable interest with so much of unusual interest to see and so many unusual things to buy and bring home as souvenirs. The people were friendly and kind and the whole trip was an amazing success. Little did these kind and gentle people know what was in store for them within months. At this time, the British Prime Minister had flown to Bertesgarten to meet Hitler in an appeasement mood and came back to England, waving a piece of paper signed by Hitler, and told us all "Peace in our time". What a worthless piece of paper this was to be. Hitler, having taken over Austria and Czechoslovakia was already planning his next conquests.

Two weeks in Malta was sufficient to service the submarines that were there at the time and it was off again to Mudros for a week before returning to Malta. Almost straight away we went on to Alexandria in the Eastern Mediterranean where we arrived on 28th September. Here we remained for two weeks, giving time to visit such exciting places as Cairo and a chance to get to know Egyptians and their customs. They appeared so inferior to us British and lived in fear of us, so very poor and so uncivilized. Not that each and every one of them would not do all that they could to deceive and swindle us. In mid-October it was back to Malta for a long stay.

The period at Malta from Mid-October until the end of February 1939 was for general refitting of the ship, painting, and smartening up, for servicing and exercising our submarines and for some relaxation for the ship's company. I took the opportunity to go to sea in one of our submarines. It was quite an experience: after leaving the harbour all hands below in preparation to dive, conning hatch closed and bolted and down we went and remained under all day, occasionally coming to periscope depth for the Captain to scan the surface and see what was about. Everyone went about their duties in the normal manner, food came, hot and steaming from the galley and apart from a complete lack of daylight there was nothing to be concerned about. By the end of the day, the air was becoming somewhat stale, but on the whole, because of the confined space and feeling of being enclosed in a sardine tin, it was pretty boring. Not something which I would want to do on a regular basis.

Whilst the wireless offices were being renovated and refitted, most of the telegraphists were transferred to Verdala Barracks where there was a Signal School and training could be continued. This was a most pleasant interlude where we had beds in small rooms of about four to a room and it was the first time I slept under a mosquito net. It was a pleasant change to sleep in a bed as opposed to a hammock anyway. We had quite good facilities to do our washing and no trouble to get the clothes dry. Food was good, all in all a most pleasant fortnight.

Another interlude was a two week stay at the gunnery range at Ghain

Tuffieha. Here too the accommodation and leisure was excellent and the daily routine vastly different to that of a normal telegraphist on board. Our training was with rifles and pistols. We learned not only how to drill with them but how to use them and I spent many happy hours on the rifle range with my .303 rifle, not that I ever became a crack shot either with rifle or pistol.

On 22nd February our rest was over and all work completed so we sailed off to Gibraltar with the rest of the Mediterranean Fleet for annual spring exercises with the Home Fleet. I was now on the opposite side and on the superior side too, but the exercises in 1939 were somewhat restricted from the normal because of the tense situation in and around Europe. In mid-March we returned to Malta for three weeks and then off to Alexandria where we set ourselves up as a base ship, not only serving the submarines but, perhaps more importantly, as a communications headquarters ship. We had excellent wireless stations at Malta and Gibraltar, but nothing of note in the Eastern Mediterranean so, of course, Maidstone was tailor made to fill this role. We became very busy and very important. In March, whilst away from Malta and the Spring Cruise / Exercises, I sat and passed the examination for Wireless Telegraphist 3. This examination was necessary for advancement to leading Telegraphist, for which I had passed educationally some years earlier. By passing this exam I could now wear a telegraphist badge with a star both above and below the wings and it brought just a little extra pay. I was 20 years old now and really not doing too badly. I was in fact fully advanced to Leading Telegraphist on 1st September whilst at Alexandria and now was a somewhat rare creature known as a "No Badge Leading Hand". The meaning of this is as follows: Good conduct badges were awarded to ratings after three years, two after seven years, and three after twelve years of good conduct. These badges were a "V" shaped stripe worn on the left arm and with them brought extra pay of 3d per day. They served no other purpose, than showing length of service. My first was due on 15th October, 1939 at the age of 21. At the same time, it was extremely unusual for any sailor to reach the rating of leading hand before the age of 21 and his first badge, this was why I was a rarity for a few weeks.

COMMENCEMENT OF WAR

It was whilst in our role of H.Q. Communications ship at Alexandria that war was declared on Germany. Hitler had invaded Poland and quite clearly was intent on taking over Europe. We gave him an ultimatum to withdraw by 11am on September 3rd or we would declare war, which we duly did. I well remember that Sunday morning in Alexandria, we were two hours in time ahead of London and had been to the usual Sunday church service on the quarter-deck, followed by lunch. Mr. Chamberlain spoke to the nation by radio just after 11am London time and of course our mess deck loud speakers were on. When he said "Consequently this nation is at war with Germany" a huge cheer went up. I was excited and kept repeating, "Let's go, let's go get at them" and the rest of my mess dubbed me "Medals Edney" for some days thereafter.

Of course, we did not go; we had a vital job to do at Alexandria and remained there until 31st October. It was now decided that our services as a communications HQ ship would be better served covering the Atlantic where German pocket battleships were roaming and sinking our merchant shipping at will, the object being to blockade Britain and starve us out. We were ordered to sail to Freetown, Sierra Leone and set ourselves up there. After brief calls at both Malta and Gibraltar (two days in each case) we anchored at Freetown in mid-November and immediately set to work with the task in hand.

This was not exactly sight-seeing or tourist country. In fact there was just nothing to see other than the mud huts in which the natives lived. There were no buildings, shops, or towns of any nature, so all of our recreational activity had to be made by ourselves on board. The climate was of course extremely hot, Freetown being situated just 7° north of the Equator. It was just work and sleep with nothing else of interest, but the period gave me an excellent opportunity to study for my educational certificate for promotion to Warrant Rank -- a long way off perhaps, but nothing like getting the qualifications behind you. I took the examination in all subjects in March. I think there was something like seven papers, in Mathematics, Geography, Naval History, English, etc., all at approximately A-level standard and am happy to say that I passed. Now I only had my technical qualifications to gain, together of course with the necessary recommendations. I just managed to complete this examination before being drafted from H.M.S. Maidstone on 14th March, back to Portsmouth for some leave and then, who knows where? In fact I had 10 days leave, after almost two years abroad and had to report to the Signal School at the R.N. Barracks

Portsmouth on 7th May 1940.

Although we had been at war for six months, by and large it had been very quiet throughout the winter. The only naval action of any significance had been the Battle of the River Plate in which three of our cruisers sank the Graf Spee -- a German armed raider who had been freely roaming the North Atlantic, sinking our shipping at will. German U-Boats had also been quite active in the North Atlantic in an endeavour to cut our life-line with the United States and Canada. To minimise this, our merchant ships were formed into convoys of up to 100 ships and escorted zig-zag across the Atlantic by destroyers; but we had insufficient destroyers for the task. The Germans began a spring offensive in no uncertain terms in April and quickly invaded Holland, Belgium, Luxembourg, as well as Norway -- they were unstoppable, the huge German machine just rolled forward. It would be quite clear that my stay at the R.N. Barracks would be short and sweet, just as I wanted it to be because a shore appointment was no place that my training and talents should be wasted. There was just time for my leave and I was allocated to H.M.S. Vanoc to be the leading Telegraphist in charge of the ship's communications.

H. M. S. VANOC

H.M.S. Vanoc was a World War I destroyer of the V+W class, built in 1917. Although classed as a destroyer in those days, she would not be a match for the present day patrol boat. Her displacement was in the order of 800 tons with one 4 inch gun forward and one aft, six torpedo tubes and depth charge throwers aft. Top speed 27 knots. The total crew including officers was about 70. The wireless office of which I was to be in charge was situated on the lower part of the bridge and consisted of two receiving sets and a very ancient arc/spark transmitter which jammed everyone else within a radius of 20 miles when used. My original communication complement was just three telegraphists.

Life aboard these ships was fairly rough to put it mildly. There was no refrigeration of any description, which meant that on leaving harbour, fresh meat had to be taken aboard and kept in the upper deck lockers. After three days, the meat was all issued or became inedible. From then on it was an issue daily of tinned meat and the only tinned meat available in 1940 was corned beef. Perhaps it is understandable why I have never eaten corned beef since those days. Much the same has to be said about bread, supplies of which again were sufficient for 3 days after which it was too stale or too mouldy and we lived on biscuits -- hard ship's biscuits, but not those from which weevils had to be shaken out first. Sanitary arrangements were somewhat primitive, and consisted of a shelter on the upper deck, fitted with a long bench containing about a dozen tin bowls. Cold water was pumped up and each man queued to fill his bowl. Showering was non-existent but a two gallon bucket of cold water was used for a bath in the open on deck The only means of obtaining hot water was from the galley where the cook kept an urn, heated from the range, for tea making purposes only. The cook was not responsible for preparing meals; his role was simply to keep the galley range burning and generally supervise the galley. The system was that at 8am daily, the cook of each mess (duty of cook was taken in turn by members of the mess) would assemble for his mess's issue of bread and meat. If it was fresh meat, it could be of any type or cut and each mess was different. If it was corned beef there was no problem. The cook of each mess was then responsible for producing a meal for the mess out of the joint he had been issued. More often than not, fresh meat was made into a hot pot or stew and corned beef into some kind of shepherd's pie if potatoes were available. It seems quite incredible now, but is a fact that the mess decks and galley were swarming with cockroaches -- not huge ones but a little larger than a fly and no one took the slightest notice of them – it would have been a waste of time anyway, there were so many, running around the table as we ate. I cannot remember how we kept ourselves warm, but never remember feeling particularly cold. We did wear plenty of clothing including the thick white roll neck submarine sweaters of which I still have one. Perhaps there were pipes running throughout the mess decks with hot water pumped through from the ship's engine room. Our sleeping quarters comprised a hammock slung in the mess decks in the usual manner.

To compensate for these conditions we were paid what was known as "hard living money", the princely sum of one shilling (5p) per day -- quite a lot in those days when the weekly payment for a leading telegraphist was in the order of 30 shillings (£1-50).

When I was appointed to Vanoc she was in Norway doing her best to assist our army stem the German offensive but, in the main, evacuating our soldiers who had been cut off. I was sent to Glasgow on 29th May where I stayed two days before being sent on to Scapa Flow to join H.M.S. Vindictive -- another destroyer of the same class, on 1st June. Vindictive sailed immediately for Norway, arriving after an uneventful journey at Harstad (Northern Norway) on 4th June. Here we met H.M.S. Vanoc, busily evacuating troops and I transferred to my permanent ship. We took the troops on to Narvik where they were to make their last stand and then spent three days patrolling and bombarding the Norwegian coast. Subsequently our troops were taken off shore to troopships for return home. The leading Telegraphist in Vanoc that I was to relieve was a real nautical character who looked as though he had been at sea with Nelson. He had a very heavy black beard and looked to me to be an old sea dog of about 60. In fact he was probably less than 40. His name was Bill Mansfield and it did not take him long to turn the reins over to me. Then he was away, probably to a troopship but I never saw nor heard of him again.

The staff that I inherited consisted of just three telegraphists, all "hostilities only". They were characters of such diversity that the details are worth including here. Firstly there was Jack Oldfield. Here was a man well into his thirties who hailed from a manor house in Sittingbourne, Kent. From a most wealthy background, he had been educated at a top public school, Marlborough or possibly Winchester. He spoke in an impeccable manner as would Royalty, never loudly, never shouting, and always in perfect English He was polite and courteous always. In peacetime he had entered politics being a member of the Greater London Council and had unsuccessfully attempted to become a Member of Parliament at the election in 1937. Oddly enough, despite his background, he was a Labour candidate and supporter, hence his entry into the Royal Navy at the outbreak of war as just an ordinary sailor, instead of as a Sub-Lieutenant which would normally have been the case for a man of his education. We became great friends and corresponded long after the war until in the 1960's he invited me down to his Manor where he was engaged in mushroom farming. Still more odd was the fact that after we had parted company, whilst in Canada, he was recalled to London to contest a political seat. He failed and then took his commission and became an officer. He also switched his allegiance from Labour to Conservative at this time.

The next member was "Dinger" Bell, a pleasant but quite uninspiring Irish lad from Belfast with a very strong Irish accent and thirdly was Ted Scott, a regular service telegraphist from Devonport depot. Lazy and lethargic would be putting it mildly. Pity really because he was a good operator, but seemed to have little interest in life or the goings on. He had marital problems also, but this would not be surprising. The four of us kept watch throughout each 24 hours on the basis of the four watch system -- a motley staff without a doubt.

Vanoc at Sullom Voe

On the 8th June, after most British troops had been evacuated, we sailed for Sullom Voe, Orkney Islands, about the most northerly point in the British Isles. The weather was fine, but a sizeable swell on the sea. Remembering that I had not been to sea in a vessel of this small size ever before, it is not surprising that I became seasick within a few hours and lay prostrate, feeling very sorry for myself in the small wireless office. On the morning of the 9th, about half way between Norway and the Orkneys we were attacked by a

German Bomber -- a Junkers 88 who straddled us with his bombs doing little damage except to blow away our aerials. This consisted of a four wire stretch from the topyard of our mainmast to the mizzen mast on "x" gun deck aft. We could not be left at sea without communications, so, seasick or otherwise, I had to get up and get on with repairs. My amazement was that although this was a communication problem, all of those aboard turned in to help, be they seamen, stokers, electricians or whatever. I had never seen this form of cooperation before on the larger ships and soon learned that this was a hallmark of life in the destroyers. Repairs were completed on the rolling ship and my seasickness disappeared rapidly, never to return on this voyage.

Our stop at Sullom Voe was brief, enough to refuel and rearm then it was off to St. Nazaire in Northern France, calling briefly at Greenock on the way. The British Army were taking a battering in France with the heavily armed Germans pushing forward on all fronts -- quite unstoppable. Our job at St. Nazaire was to evacuate as many of the British troops as we could and get them aboard troopships for return home. At the same time, in the English Channel, a mass evacuation was taking place at Dunkirk, where a miracle was achieved in getting the majority of our troops home. During our evacuation at St. Nazaire, we had just completed loading one troopship, with some 1000 or more soldiers when she was bombed and sunk by German Aircraft -- I believe one bomb went straight down her funnel and blew her to pieces. How many survivors there were I do not know, but not many I suspect. The job was completed by 18th June when we returned to Plymouth, for a break, to get our breath back and await further developments. Seemingly, relatively quiet, we were sent to Liverpool on 1st July for convoy duty.

Whilst operating from Liverpool during July and August, I took the opportunity to pass the examination for W/T2 (Wireless Telegraphist 2nd grade.) This was the qualification required technically for advancement to Petty Officer Telegraphist, the educational examination having been obtained in my days aboard H.M.S. Nelson in 1936. This particular examination was of a lower standard than that required normally and would only allow for my promotion in due course on a temporary basis. It would be necessary for me to have a training course in the Signal School to take the full examination and of course I could not be spared from my duties at this stage for several weeks at H.M.S. Mercury (Petersfield).

This was not to be for long. Following the evacuation of the British Army from France, it was widely expected that Hitler's next move would be to cross the English Channel, invade England and take it over. We had lost a fair proportion of our army and most of our tanks and weapons and were not really in a position to repulse an invader. Nothing however happened until early September when the German Luftwaffe attempted to take control of the air. They met more than they bargained for against the few pilots that we had left and their Spitfires. The Battle of Britain was fought and won by the few and so, in the event, our country saved. In the meantime, it was our duty at sea to prevent landing craft crossing with troops to land along our South Coast. So, on 8th September we were assigned to the Anti-Invasion Patrol in the English Channel, constantly on patrol from Dover to Isle of Wight and refuelling as necessary at Portsmouth or Southampton. By 28th September, the immediate invasion scare was over and we settled ourselves in Portsmouth alternating between immediate notice and four hours' notice to sail.

This gave an opportunity for certain modifications to be done, in all departments, but particularly the wireless department. We had our old and useless arc/spark transmitter taken out and a new modern set installed. We also had RADAR fitted, primitive though it was compared with later installations. Depth charges and throwers had to be fitted, plus anti-submarine equipment, and so many other up to date modifications made. It also gave me the opportunity to get home to Bognor and see my family when we were at four hours' notice for sailing. The train journey to Bognor was about one hour. I frequently took Jack Oldfield with me which, looking back, must have frightened my mother to death. To me he was just a colleague but I fear my mother must have been full of apprehension. However we went and enjoyed ourselves. My brother and I used to delight in getting Jack down to the Pavilion for roller skating. He couldn't skate of course but we would get him on the rink and push him until he fell. We had great fun but I don't know whether he thought so. We were at sea from time to time, doing anti-submarine or depth charge trials, sometimes escorting a convoy through the channel. Throughout this, whilst at immediate notice, we had our wireless watches to keep. On 9th January whilst in harbour, bombs were dropped, close to the ship and on 10th we moved out to Spithead. Just as well as on that night the Air Blitz on Portsmouth took place and the town was still burning on 11th.

On 19th January I was granted a week's leave and went to Liverpool to see a girl whom I had met there during our spell of convoy duty between July and September the previous year and with whom I had maintained communication by letter. I would have stayed in one of the service hostels, probably the Union Jack Club, which was quite comfortable. Some time was spent with Doris at the cinema or the Grafton Dance Hall. Some I spent on my own going to the great Liverpool Empire Hall. On return from leave my new transmitter and RADAR had been fitted and I spent many hours with the Warrant Telegraphist of the dockyard, tuning it, followed by RADAR trials at sea. By 5th February we were ready and left Portsmouth for Liverpool in very rough seas which caused me to be quite seasick.

We arrived at Liverpool on the 7th February and sailed with our convoy on the 9th. These convoy trips lasted about ten days. After leaving Liverpool we would stop at Londonderry to refuel as we could not operate more than ten days without refuelling again. Consequently we would take an outbound convoy for five days and reach almost half way across the Atlantic, then pick up the homeward convoy. The speed of the convoy was that of the slowest ship and at best was six knots on an irregular zig-zag course to avoid torpedoes from U-Boats. We travelled more than twice the distance that would be required for sailing direct. The weather was often rough, uncomfortable, cold and unpleasant, but the job had to be done to keep our island fed and clothed. The respite in harbour varied between 2 or 3 days to a week, depending on what maintenance was required to be done on board. Obviously we all made the most of our time in port by getting ashore whenever possible, going dancing, drinking, or visiting the shows or a cinema.

Vanoc after Atlantic gale

On 7th November 1940, I was promoted to Acting Petty Officer Telegraphist (temporary) on the basis of the examination I had pressed in August. I was just 22 and not far from my ultimate ambition of Chief Petty Officer, with 18 years yet to serve. This promotion meant that I would remain in sailor's uniform, (not the square rig of confirmed Petty Officers) but wear the appropriate insignia on my right arm, together with my good conduct stripe received at the age of 21. At this time, it was almost unheard of for a rating with less than eight years' service to be a petty officer, but the war had helped and I did it in four years. The most satisfying part of this promotion was that I moved from the sailors' mess deck, in the bows of the ship to the petty officers mess, a much more civilized mess, completely separate and consisting of around eight other petty officers. It also meant that I could now partake of my daily issue of rum, neat, i.e. without water added.

Rum was a daily issue to all seamen not of commissioned officer rank, over the age of 21. For the sailors it was diluted, three of water to one full tot of rum. It had to be consumed on the spot of issue, 12 noon daily. Alternatively, those who did not want a rum issue could be paid four pence daily. I found the concoction insipid and elected for the extra pay. However as a Petty Officer with neat rum available I chose the rum which was "lifting" to take and, although illegal, could be bottled as it would keep. Mostly I drank mine daily, bearing in mind that eight full tots was the equivalent of a full bottle of spirits.

Another concession of the navy was a monthly issue of tobacco or cigarettes. This amounted to one pound of tobacco, either pipe or cigarette, or 500 previously rolled cigarettes. There was a small charge for this, but it was negligible as it was duty free. There was also an issue of leaf tobacco in lieu, if required. This was the plain tobacco leaf, which the old salts rolled tightly and bound with tarred hemp, what was known as a "prick" and was subsequently cut in thin slices to smoke in a pipe. Guaranteed to make any normal youngster violently sick, it was a dying art - none of the navy could take that. For my part I did not bother drawing my tobacco issue, sensibly knowing it was no good for me.

Now, the most momentous event of my life was about to happen. On Sunday 9th, I went ashore with Jack Oldfield for drinks at a pub and then on for a meal at the rather elite Exchange Hotel. On Monday 10th I was invited to join Jack, the canteen manager and Paul, the ship's supply petty officer to go with them to the Grafton, for a blind date. It was not a blind date for them - they had met a couple of girls, Iris and Esther, the previous time in port and had been invited to Iris' birthday party on the 24th February. Iris had a sister, Thelma, who appeared to be unattached at the time although she was rather young at just 17. It was agreed that Iris and Esther would bring Thelma along to the Grafton and Jack and Paul would take me, to make up the six. Needless to say, we had a great time. I found Thelma, very lively, very entertaining and most attractive with a tremendous personality and sex appeal. I plied her with drink, in which she had not imbibed before at her young age, and then escorted her home by tram to Stoneycroft. The following day I met her again and took her home where her very kind parents gave me a bed for the night, returning to Vanoc the following morning. I again met her later that day and we went to the cinema. There was quite a heavy air raid on Liverpool whist we were in the cinema, but we sat through it all and then had to walk home all the way from Lime Street in the centre of Liverpool to Stoneycroft -- about 5 miles out, as there was no transport running. Many a time on that long walk home did we drop flat on our faces on the pavement as the bombs dropped, but we made it quite uninjured. It had been a lovely four days in harbour and when we sailed with the next convoy on 13th March, I was very happy.

The next convoy escort duty began, as had most others quite peacefully in a very calm sea up through the Irish Sea to Londonderry for the usual refuelling. Little did we know what was ahead of us. We

Thelma & Walter 1941

wasted little time in Londonderry and sailed again at almost full speed, 20 knots, to pick up a convoy. The sea remained calm. During the night of 14th, although we had not met the convoy, it was reported that one of their number, a tanker, had been torpedoed. We finally reached them at on Sat 15th in mid-Atlantic and joined H.M.S. Walker to bring the convoy home. During the night that followed, a Sunday night, four more ships of the convoy had been torpedoed by midnight and it became clear that U-Boats were operating among this convoy, surfacing and firing torpedoes at will. What use could two First World War destroyers be amongst this, for that was all of which the escort consisted. Just after midnight, Walker sighted the fluorescent wash of a U-Boat retreating on the surface and immediately gave chase, dropping a pattern of depth charges (10) over the likely diving position of the U-Boat. Unfortunately contact was lost, the U-Boat disappeared and Walker steamed to pick up survivors from yet another tanker. What was not known, was the fact that the U-Boat had been damaged by the depth charges and, unable to stay under water for long periods,. it decided to surface for inspection of the damage. As it did so, my RADAR operator immediately reported a dark green blob which he thought might be a U-Boat. The fact was reported to H.M.S. Walker and both ships then raced at top speed along the bearing given by the RADAR operator. After a little more than a mile, the silhouette of a U-Boat could be seen on the surface, so without hesitation our Captain gave the order "Stand by to ram." This we did, in no uncertain manner, at full speed, hitting the U-Boat amidships and toppling her over. It brought Vanoc to a sudden standstill, embedded in the U-Boat which was only cleared by both engines, full astern. The U-Boat rose high in the air and sunk, the Captain

H.M.S. Walker laying a smoke-screen

still on the bridge wearing his white cap but badly injured went down with her. There were few survivors, just five from a crew of 50 who had probably jumped over-board before the collision

It subsequently transpired that the U-Boat we had sunk was U100, captained by a Lieut. Capt. Joachim Schepke, a U-Boat Ace who had sunk many thousand tons of British shipping. A further observation of this action that perhaps made history was the fact that this was the first time that such a primitive and crude RADAR set had led to the attack on a U-Boat, remembering that the set had only been installed a few months before and that the aerial had to be rotated manually.

We next swept the surface of the waters with our searchlight in order to pick up survivors. I well remember and will do so always, the cries of those men in the icy waters "Camerade." In my youth, my bitterness towards them was extreme; they had sunk our ships and many of our seamen drowned at sea. Their air force (the Luftwaffe) had bombed our cities relentlessly killing thousands of innocent civilians. I just had to shout "Leave them there." Fortunately perhaps the older members of our crew had more compassion and pulled up the side as many as they could, before the next alarm. It had amounted to just five, one officer and four men

Whilst recovering these survivors the Walker ASDIC operator reported a U-Boat echo which, on investigation, placed it directly under our stern, where we were stopped recovering survivors. There was only one answer, to get away quickly and depth charge, which we did, followed by a run over the spot by H.M.S. Walker who also dropped a bank of depth charges. Any further swimmers that may have been in the water, and there were some, could not possibly have survived this fierce attack. After a short while, a U-Boat surfaced just astern of us, so close that it was necessary to move out of the way fairly quickly for fear of being torpedoed or fired upon. It was not to be, in fact both Walker and Vanoc opened a cross fire at the U-Boat, with nothing in reply and no movement from the U-Boat. It was quite clear that she was badly damaged and the crew would have to surrender. The U-Boat flashed a message in English to Walker to the effect that she was sinking. The bow of the U-Boat subsequently rose in the air and she slithered down to her grave. The whole of the crew took to the water, all saved, including the captain, with the exception of the Engineer Officer and two seamen.

What we had achieved! This was U-99, captained by Lieut. Cmdr. Otto Kretschmer, the unchallenged Ace of the German U-Boat fleet after Prien who had been sunk with his U-Boat a few days before by H.M.S. Wolverine -- another of the old V+W class. But what of ourselves? The damage to our bow was extensive, but the water tight doors were holding and the engines were sound, we would be of little use but we remained with the convoy at slow speed and left them for Loch Ewe, Scotland on the morning of 18th. We had to leave at this point because we were desperately short of fuel, having steamed at high speed to meet the convoy and used much full power during the action. It took three hours to refuel and we left to re-join the convoy for Liverpool, but did not proceed into harbour as usual. We anchored outside the bay in the Mersey. The following day, which by now was 20th March, we proceeded up harbour at 11am, to be met by the Admiral of Western Approaches and much other top brass. Here we received congratulations all round, discharged our prisoners, and settled ourselves in Gladstone Dock for what was to be a period of repairs to our bow, among other modifications. In due course, many months later, awards were made for this action, our own Captain and the Captain of Walker were both awarded the Distinguished Service Cross, our ASDIC operator the Distinguished Service Medal and for my part, not that I know what it was, I received a mention in dispatches. I suppose my part had been keeping sound and efficient communications including the

At work on H.M.S. Vanoc

RADAR which was my responsibility. A good account of this action is given in a book entitled "The Golden Horseshoe" by Terence Robertson.

Well the first thing for me to do on return to Liverpool was to call and see Thelma, which I did without delay. I had a good hot bath at her home, went out and got very drunk. We were going to be in dock some time for repairs, so leave was immediately granted for two weeks although I did not go myself until a week later. There was work to do on board before we docked and the "Dockies" took over -- dismantling certain transmitters, taking down wireless aerials, and rewiring the radio office, but I was able to get ashore each evening and be with Thelma. As before we would spend our evenings at the Grafton, dancing, or go to the cinema or even, on a Sunday, picnic in North Wales. Thelma was working of course. I frequently stayed overnight in her home and her parents treated me as though I was their own son. I had meals provided, hot baths, and all home comforts, which considering they were on strict rations, was more than exceptionally good of them and which I very much appreciated.

Thelma's parents were two of the nicest people I have had the good fortune to meet and know in my life. Her father, Ernie, was in the Liverpool Police as a plain clothes detective on dock duties. His job was to board ships and interview their Captains. He had descended from very good stock, his grandfather and great grandfather having been officers of substantial rank in the army whilst his father had been Lay Preacher at Chichester, Chester and other Cathedrals. For reasons which I cannot go into here, he had fallen on difficult times and left home to join the Army in the First World War where he served with distinction in the Medical Corps, being awarded the Conspicuous Gallantry Medal. He was a perfect gentleman in every sense, so humorous, bright and cheerful. I regarded him a very great friend and respect and admire him more than anyone else I have ever met. Her mother was a perfect lady in every sense. Although unfortunately deaf, since her childhood, she never let this affliction interfere with or spoil her life. She too had descended from good stock; one of her forbears was the Earl of Lathom and, like her husband, had qualities of good society and never flagged in her standards until her death at the age of 93, although she had lived as a widow for 25 years by that time. She had her own 3 children, nine grandchildren and seventeen great-grandchildren at her death. Never once did she forget a birthday and a present for each of them, although she had merely a state pension and small police pension on which to live. Not once during the 48 years that I knew her did we have a cross word, nor for that matter did I ever fall out with Ernie.

With two parents such as these, Thelma's home was a very happy one, no unpleasantness at any time, just politeness and good manners. There would be few homes of such harmony, even though the home was a modest council home in what was then the better part of Liverpool. Iris, the elder sister was two and a half years older than Thelma and Mavis, the youngest some nine years her junior. Iris subsequently married one of my telegraphists from Vanoc and lived a happy life with him. Mavis married a local boy, the marriage lasted but a few years and after a divorce, Mavis lived on her own, ably supported for many years by her mother.

So much for Thelma's family background. Our vessel was soon moved to Birkenhead and dry docked for repairs. Home leave was granted and I made for the South in order to visit my parents. I spent most of the time out with my brother, to cinemas or the roller skating rink or perhaps to the pub with my father. I also took the opportunity of visiting my cousin in Mitcham and relations in Brentwood who were rather better placed than my own parents. All in all, I had a very nice two weeks leave and a lovely girl to return to in Liverpool. There was not a great deal that could be done on board whilst dockyard repairs were taking place and life there was not at all comfortable. Consequently the opportunity was taken for plenty of home leave. Late in April, I applied for my full qualifying course for P.O. Telegraphist, for which I would have to attend the Signal School, now at Petersfield, Hants. In late April I had a further week's leave and took Thelma to my home in Bognor to meet my parents. I think she found my home somewhat different to her own and was probably glad to leave when I saw her off on the train a week later. I went directly from this leave to the Signal School at Petersfield.

Actually it was a disastrous trip home for Thelma. When she eventually arrived in Liverpool, there had been the most terrible bombing of the city the previous night. The city was ablaze, with thousands of refugees trampling out carrying what little belongings they could salvage. They were making their way to the outskirts, or anywhere away from the burning city. Thelma was terrified of course, but joined the refugees. She had no choice, eventually arriving home, footsore and weary to see most of the houses in her street had been bombed flat. She was sure that her home and her family were gone. In the event, it was the houses opposite to her own which had taken the hit and her mother and sister were safe though severely shaken. Her father was missing. He had been on police duty in the city the previous night – fire watching from the roofs of buildings and it was not known whether he had survived. Fortunately he did, for he turned up home, many hours later, blackened and dishevelled, but safe.

I next spent two weeks of intense study at Petersfield during which I was informed that I was to be drafted to H.M.S. Talybont, a new small escort destroyer which had just completed building. This worried me intensely. Quite clearly Vanoc was not entitled to a fully qualified petty officer, but it probably meant for me that my days of operating from Liverpool and seeing Thelma would have to come to an end. I remonstrated and so did my officers from Vanoc, on my behalf, so the draft was not enforced and I was allowed to stay. Consequently I returned to Vanoc in mid-May. Repairs to the ship were finally completed by mid-June and we sailed on the 19th for Londonderry where we carried out trials of all the new equipment and fully tested everything, bringing ourselves back to fighting fitness again. We had one week of working up trials. Whilst in dock, I had got together with the ship's gunner - a petty officer who had a gunnery station on the upper deck. I had to have some of my new wireless equipment fitted into his office, which backed on to my wireless office. We had built for ourselves a pair of bunks in what was known as the Transmitting Station and from now on, our sleeping arrangements would be quite civilized. We sailed to collect our next convoy from Greenock on 24th June. Meanwhile the results of my examination came through - I had passed, top of the class and was able to drop the "Temporary" from my title.

The next three months were spent on convoy escort duty, each trip lasting seven to ten days with usually three days in harbour at Liverpool. Ships of the convoy were repeatedly sunk, sometimes, but not always, survivors were rescued by the escorting destroyers. Frequently depth

Survivors from "Ortio"

charges were dropped when a suspected SONAR contact was obtained but there was never confirmation of any further U-Boat sinkings. Sometimes the convoy was attacked by aircraft and bombing raids carried out. Convoy ships were hit but not sunk by aircraft attacks. We formed a ship's football team to play other escort destroyers during the brief periods in harbour and I was able to see Thelma at frequent intervals. It was a quiet and somewhat boring period, but we were doing an important job and getting the convoys through. There was no way Hitler was going to starve us out. Meanwhile he had missed his opportunity to invade, whilst we were rearming and re-equipping at breakneck speed with the help of the U.S.A.

In October there was a slight change to our normal routine when we were able to leave an outward bound convoy in mid-Atlantic and proceed to Iceland for refuelling. Our first visit was on the 1st October for three days. This lengthened the time for each trip, but it was a pleasure to be able to get fresh provisions half way through a convoy trip. These visits to Iceland (Reykjavik) continued on into December, sometimes in the roughest of weathers -- the seas can be very unkind in that part of the world in late autumn and winter. Our football team was very active during this period, never missing the opportunity to play, be it in Liverpool or Reykjavik. I gave up my position as goalkeeper for the team which I found either quite boring and cold standing around or as being an "Aunt Sally" for the opposing team playing in mid-field.

On 10th December Vanoc entered Liverpool for a slightly longer break than normal in order to give each watch seven days leave. We were due to sail again on 21st December so would not be home for Christmas. I stayed at the seaman's hostel in Liverpool in order to see as much of Thelma as possible, which I did -- every day. By this time I had decided that I would like Thelma for my wife and we discussed the matter. After some gentle persuasion, she agreed, but would set no firm date for the engagement, although she agreed to come with me and select a ring. This was surprising really as our relationship had been far from smooth, quite the contrary. There had been more arguments and sulking than there had been happy periods, but underneath it all was a love on both sides I believe. On Monday 15th December we both went into Liverpool to do Christmas shopping and looked at various engagement rings in jewellers until we found the one Thelma liked -- not gold but platinum, with two rather lovely diamonds inset. I said she would not see it again until our engagement day. We went to Reece's in the centre of Liverpool, upstairs to the tea rooms for tea and cakes, during which Thelma asked to see the ring again. I said "No, not unless we become engaged now." She finally submitted, said she would, and I produced the ring and placed it on her finger. She was thrilled, I was thrilled, but I don't know if her parents were -- their permission had never been sought, but, such as they are, they accepted the situation and wished us well. After the greatest leave ever, I returned aboard the ship sailed for Londonderry on the 21st.

Monday 22nd saw us on our way to meet a convoy which was being attacked by U-Boats, but on the 23rd we were ordered to chase, catch, and sink a German tanker, now close to the north coast of Spain. On this day we were attacked by two Junkers 88 bombers, but managed to get away without damage. The situation by evening however, was that due to our high speed in the chase we were running seriously short of fuel. For some reason or other, we discovered later that a signal from the Admiralty, ordering us home at 4am had not been received. Now we were ordered to proceed to Gibraltar. Christmas day was spent in a very calm sea and we made the most of our Christmas dinner, albeit corned beef, concocted into a dish. My diary says "Very nice dinner". It was extremely doubtful at this stage whether or not we would make Gibraltar, due to the fuel running so low, however we did make it by 2pm on Boxing Day with just 1.5 hours fuel remaining -- a near thing.

Stationed in Gibraltar at the same time was H.M.S. Maidstone, my previous ship and I wasted no time going aboard to visit some of my old shipmates that were still there. I had left them eighteen months before as a very junior Leading Telegraphist and was now a Petty Officer. What is more, my Petty Officer rating had been confirmed in full in November, so I was no longer wearing a sailor's uniform, but what was known as "square rig" -- shirt, tie, jacket, trousers, and peaked cap. Anyway it was nice to see them again and to go ashore to the various bars in Gibraltar with them. Needless to say, as always on these occasions we had more than enough to drink.

The morning of the 30th I spent aboard M.V. Batory, in conference reference sailing, which we did at 6pm in calm seas. We made our way to Milford Haven, where we arrived with this vessel of some importance at 2am, January 4th. Our stop here was to be short, just enough to refuel and sail again at 11am with another important vessel for the Clyde. This duty completed on 5th January we turned and set sail for Liverpool arriving on 6th to be greeted by masses and masses of Christmas mail and for me to dash ashore to Thelma's home. During these few days respite, Thelma and I arranged an engagement party for Friday 9th January, although her parents had all the work and expense. At this party I invited all of my staff from Vanoc, including Jackie Oldfield and Fred

Telegraphist crew of H.M.S. Vanoc 1941

Chilton who had been with us for some months. It was here that Fred met Thelma's sister -- Iris, subsequently to wed and live a long and happy married life. We received very many engagement presents, Jackie Oldfield made a very pleasant speech and we all had a wonderful evening running into the early hours of the next morning. All stayed overnight, sleeping on the floor or wherever a space could be found. Back on board the following day, we sailed with our next convoy and returned on the 18th January.

It was now decided that escorts further afield in the Atlantic needed strengthening. Consequently, together with several other "V" class destroyers, we sailed with convoy from Liverpool on the 25th February, crossing the Atlantic, reaching St. John's in Newfoundland 4th March and from there on to Halifax (Canada.) From here we were on escort duties, taking us to Boston (U.S.A.) and, in May, down to Bermuda for a short refit in Bermuda dockyard. Bermuda was to be a haven of peace and rest for us for a month. We had a week away from the ship, camping out in the beautiful islands and occupied ourselves with football, shooting, fishing, sailing, etc. It was a sad day when we had to leave, but the war was still raging and so in June it was back to Halifax where, until September, we worked with convoys along the American coast, visiting Newport and Boston on a number of occasions. Our visits to the U.S. cities were a revelation. In Halifax it was good but in the U.S., out of this world. Shops and stores packed full of goods the likes of which we had never seen at home, especially with a war on. Needless to say we shopped with all the money at our disposal for goods to bring home. One item that I remember in particular was some 20 yards of pure white satin which I wanted to bring home for Thelma's wedding dress.

In Early September we left Halifax for St. John's, Newfoundland to collect a convoy and make our way back home, leaving St. John's on the 16th September. Two days out of St. Johns ships in the convoy were being sunk by U-Boats, a not unusual event. H.M.S. Vindictive, an accompanying destroyer, obtained a sonar contact on a U-Boat and left the convoy to investigate further. She was never seen again, sunk at night with all hands by torpedo -- we knew nothing of it, other than our concern when she did not re-join us and we could make no contact with her by radio. A sad loss of many of our friends. This was the ship that had taken me from Glasgow to join Vanoc. Eventually we reached Liverpool on 1st October after our usual refuelling at Londonderry. Now came the problem of getting all our goodies, purchased in the United States, ashore without paying too much to the Customs Authorities. Many items were honestly declared, but I did not wish to pay duty on the yards of satin I had purchased. I wrapped it around and around my body and dressed over it, looking considerably more portly than I would normally. Dressed in this fashion, I waltzed through the dock gates, past the dock police, my heart pounding, but I was not stopped and got my valuable purchase back to Thelma's home for her dress to be designed and made. Fortunately her mother was a qualified dress maker so there would be no problem in this respect.

Our stay in Liverpool was to be short-lived. We were now required for convoy escort duties in the Mediterranean, so, on 16th October we sailed to Gibraltar, where, until the end of 1942 we escorted convoys along the North African coast, visiting Algeria, Oran, Casablanca, but never as far as

Malta, now under siege by the Germans but holding out valiantly. It needed more up to date destroyers than ours to penetrate and sustain the attacks delivered on Malta convoys. One unfortunate incident occurred whilst alongside the harbour wall in Gibraltar during this period. The warship ahead of us was engaged in cleaning its Bofors gun, aft. I was standing on the Port Waist at the top of the forecastle ladder discussing some matter with the ship's communications officer, an Australian Lieutenant RNR. There was a huge explosion just above my head, the Bofors gun in the vessel ahead had been accidentally fired and the shell struck the stanchion just above my head. Splinters of metal flew everywhere penetrating the chest of Lieut. Knott who staggered back, fell down the ladder and was, sadly, killed. I was more fortunate, one piece (as far as I know) of shrapnel penetrated my head, near to the brain, but not deep enough to cause damage. Many weeks later it worked its way to the surface and came away of its own accord. A very small piece I am happy to say.

PROMOTION, WEDDING AND HONEYMOON

By January 1943 my time in Vanoc had to come to an end and I was to be relieved and sent home for other things. My successor arrived, I turned over to him and then joined H.M.S. Tanantside for transport home. I arrived at Devonport on the 22nd January from where I went to the Signal School at Portsmouth and then on to H.M.S. Mercury, the Communications training centre at Leydene, near Petersfield. I was here but a short time when I was informed that I had been selected for the next Warrant Telegraphists course. Immediately, I was instructed to report to the Sick Bay for medical examination. I could not get there quick enough. I was reported medically fit, except for slightly high blood pressure -- no doubt caused by the excitement of this undreamed of selection. I was perhaps fearful of those with whom I would share the course -- their knowledge, background, and all more experienced than I. But I was determined to do well and to pass.

The course lasted until Friday 10th July, by which time all final exams had been completed in eleven subjects. My results were of the highest, totalling to be top of the class. Now it was time for some leave and, in fact, our marriage which had been arranged for July 17th. The course had been great fun, the company great and the feeling of superiority great! Although petty officers, we had the honour of falling in for daily divisions, with the remainder of the establishment, quite separately -- not quite with the officers, but certainly separated from all remaining petty offer and ratings, as special people.

I now had to change my uniform for an officer's uniform and spent a few days at the Naval Tailors being fitted out with the many items required including sword, belt, trunk, etc., etc. I discarded my Petty Officer's kit and felt so proud and smart in an officer's uniform with one thin gold stripe on each sleeve. Later in the week it was on to Liverpool to join Thelma and make final preparations for the wedding which duly took place on a lovely sunny Saturday afternoon.

Thelma looked gorgeous in her wedding dress, veil, and bouquet of flowers -- absolutely radiant. I was dressed in my new officer's uniform. The church was full. I added a highlight to the service by responding "I do" to the vicar when he asked "Wilt thou take this woman to be thy lawfully wedded wife" -- he quietly corrected me to say "I will." The reception was held on the first floor of Reece's in the centre of Liverpool and a great spread was provided for a large number of guests. Thelma's parents did us well although I doubt that we appreciated it at the time. In the evening we left for our honeymoon which was to be in the Isle of Man, leaving Liverpool (Lime Street) for Fleetwood at 8pm. We had a marvellous send off from all the guests who came down to the platform. Someone got the guard to lock our carriage door, so that no one else could get into the same carriage. I don't know how we were expected to get out or how in fact we ever did get out -- the guard must have returned at some stage to release us, probably at Fleetwood. From Fleetwood we caught the Isle of Man ferry and eventually arrived at our hotel in Douglas, quite late and ready for bed.

I had been granted 14 days leave and had to report back to

Wedding Day

the RN Barracks, Portsmouth on 25th July. This allowed for just 6 days in the Isle of Man which we enjoyed to the full under the wartime conditions. Thelma came to Portsmouth with me, after a brief call at her home on the way through Liverpool. On arrival, we booked into the top hotel in Southsea for the night. It was expected Thelma would look for suitable accommodation the next day and I reported to the barracks at 9am. I don't think Thelma had much luck, not knowing where to start, but one of the newly qualified officers from my course, who lived in Portsmouth, gave me an address at which we called in the evening and were given a room. It was pretty low class accommodation, not at all the standard Thelma was used to, but at least a bed, until we could sort ourselves out -- and so began married life. In actual fact we were left little time to sort ourselves out as I was fairly soon appointed to be the Warrant Telegraphist in charge of communications for a Naval Port party -- a landing party to set up in captured ports. I was to join the port party at Devonport on 8th August. We therefore felt Thelma would be better off back in her own home whilst I got on with the business of the war -- we had 10 happy but hard days together after our honeymoon – little did I know at this time that I would not see her again for two and a half years.

I duly travelled to RNB Devonport on 7th August and assembled with the port party on the 8th. This party of about 200 men were to be ready to take over a port as soon as the Army had captured it and to clear up the devastation to get it operating again. This would mean clearing all mines, both from the harbour and ashore, clearing rubble left from the fighting, getting power and water facilities restored and establishing communications with the outside world —— which was my responsibility, for which I was allocated a team of telegraphists. The Americans had been brought into the war in Dec. 1941 by the ruthless bombing of the U.S. Navy at Pearl Harbour when a substantial portion of their fleet was sunk. The Japanese had taken all territory as far as and including Singapore and were pushing their way up through Burma, towards India. The Germans had smashed through to Tobruk in Libya and were well on their way to Egypt. It was anyone's guess as to which theatre of the war we were to be sent, certainly there were plenty of possibilities and a lot of fighting to be done.

PORT LANDING PARTY - INDIA

After twenty four hours in Devonport, the whole party boarded a train and arrived the next day at Liverpool to join the M/V Monarch of Bermuda, still unaware of our destination. Within forty eight hours we sailed to the Clyde to form up with a convoy and then on 16th August sailed in a Southerly direction towards the Mediterranean. In fact we reached Suez on the 30th August where we transferred to M/V Ascania and sailed on through the Canal and the Red-Sea to Aden. It was clear now that we were destined for the Far Eastern theatre. At Aden we again transferred to a sister ship of the Aseania -- M/V Ascania and wasted no time in setting off for Bombay which we reached on 14th Sept. Here we disembarked. I well remember my arrival in Bombay -- I went on deck to watch the milling crowds of Indians on the jetty. On returning to my cabin a few moments later, my wallet with every penny of my cash was well and truly gone - I was penniless and devastated. It was a hard lesson but one that remained with me for life. Never leave anything unguarded and trust no one, although there was no doubt that it had been stolen by Indians who had boarded the ship. At Bombay officers were accommodated in the Taj Mahal Hotel, very comfortable in every way and we were soon at training for the task ahead. I was given a rather large motor caravan affair which was fitted out with radio receivers and a transmitter, plus all equipment to maintain them. Additionally and rather more unusual was a large sectionalized mast with which we had great fun while learning to erect. I suppose it was some fifty feet in height and made of steel. The bottom part was fitted steel and of a tripod nature, the remainder was vertical poles, the whole thing being held by steel guys. We would erect, communicate, and dismantle every day, until we could do the whole thing confidently and with speed. In Bombay Thelma had an uncle (Harry) who was an executive with Unilever, quite high up in their Bombay headquarters. He lived, together with his wife, Kay, in the Yacht Club of Bombay -- the most exclusive club in this great city. Harry and Kay were good to me whilst I was there, frequently taking me on outings and inviting me into the Yacht club from which an officer of my lowly rank would have been barred. Before leaving Bombay I left with them for safe keeping the gold watch given to me by my parents on my 21st birthday. It was of tremendous sentimental value to me. They cared for it and eventually brought it back to England where I received it at the end of the war. I still have it.

Oddly enough, our stay in Bombay was not lengthy. The Americans under General MacArthur had now commenced a major offensive in the Far East and those under General Eisenhower in the Mediterranean were pushing the Germans back through Libya. At the same time the British Eighth Army had landed in Sicily and was poised to cross the straits of Messina into Italy. The Italians had no hesitation in surrendering when they saw the position, leaving the Germans to hold back the U.S. Fifth Army and British Eighth I think the decision had been taken to end the European battles before concentrating on the Far-East and that our Port Party would be of more use to Eisenhower than MacArthur. At Christmas 1943 we therefore embarked again and sailed back to the Mediterranean, via Suez -- to Naples.

The Allies had made swift movement up through Italy but Rome would be a problem. It was felt, that by encircling Rome, no damage would come to this city and all Germans to the South would have to capitulate. Landings were therefore made at Anzio, a port to the North-West of Rome and a beachhead was established in late January 1944. I paid a visit to Anzio for twenty four hours on 29th January to establish the position as far as communications was concerned, hoping that it would not be necessary for our team to go. Back in Naples, training continued with visits to a number of attractive places to set up and establish communications, among them Ischia and Ponza. However by April the beachhead was still being contained at Anzio where fierce fighting was taking place.

Our party was to go and take over the port which we did on 10th April. It was a very interesting experience with the Germans surrounding us on one side about 5 miles away and the sea on the other. They bothered us little really apart from the odd shells arriving at the most unexpected times. We sat there and held them off until Rome was captured, but never did succeed with the original plan. Life was pretty rough here, living in dilapidated buildings, war torn, no power or water except for that which we produced ourselves. The officer's toilets were in a long shed -- one long bench with holes in it for seating, raised above the ground and a pit underneath. Quite an experience, but not exactly a salubrious one. It was goodbye to Anzio and back to Naples on 31st May after just six weeks. Life back in Naples seemed just wonderful after Anzio, but training continued as before, including a visit to the recently captured Rome on the 19th June.

In July, with the allies still advancing through Italy, we moved up the coast to the port of Leghorn (Livomo). Here I was to spend a whole year in comparative comfort doing nothing except keeping myself and team up to peak efficiency. Here I met and became friendly with a young Italian girl employed at Naval Headquarters as Captain's Secretary. She was only 18, named Iolanda, but became a great help to me showing me around the country. I had volunteered to be the wardroom mess caterer, in which capacity I was responsible for purchasing wines. Iolanda would take me into the countryside where I met and she bargained for wines. Always we had a meal of the most delicious Palma Ham, home cooked of course. At one place, for a pair of old army boots, a local character carved for me a bust of Thelma in alabaster from a photograph. These were really great days, we visited Pisa and the Leaning Tower, Via Regio, a seaside resort and Genoa after it had been captured. I had a boring trip to Genoa to keep in touch with communications, visiting four times in May and June for short periods. From here I was able to visit Milan and Lake Como. During this period the allied forces opened up what was known as the second front on the continent of Europe. In June 1944 mass landings by the British, Americans, and many other nations were made on the beaches of Normandy, a bridgehead secured and soon our troops were pushing forward towards Paris. By April 1945 the Germans capitulated. Berlin was captured and Hitler committed suicide. There now seemed nothing more for our Port Party to do and so we were disbanded, although it was September before I was reappointed to Headquarters in Malta. Once again there was little for me to do and so I worked to be sent home and eventually arrived back at Devonport, by troopship, on 15th November some 2 years and four months after I had left.

It took me very little time to leave the troopship, take all my kit and go down to Devonport station for a train to Liverpool. I was unable to contact Thelma to let her know that I was on my way because her parents were not connected by telephone, nor did I know of anyone who was, that might be able to give her a message. I just remember arriving at Wavertree station very late at night with everything deserted and quiet and as far as I know, no taxi available probably due to the chronic shortage of petrol in the aftermath of the war. Presumably I left my kit in the left luggage office to be collected the next day and walked from Wavertree to Stoneycroft -- Thelma's home. Not exactly a war hero's welcome home as happens these days after a skirmish somewhere in the world, but then no one had such a welcome home in those days.

Certainly there was a great welcome awaiting me in Anstey Road, and in due course I was able to go to bed with my wife of two and a half years, with whom I had spent only two weeks to date. My leave commenced, ending officially, sometime after Christmas, but as an officer, I remained on leave until it was time to take up my next appointment which came in February 1946. During this period the weather was not at its best, rain, cold, and snow and Thelma continued with her job. I spent some of the time dismantling the corrugated iron air raid shelter in the back garden. It had been dug into the ground and took quite a bit of digging out I was, however, young and full of energy. I had my parents to visit in Bognor and other various relations to see as well as calls at the Admiralty to find out when I could expect another appointment, so the time passed with no difficulties.

The appointment came in February, to join H.M.S. Sheffield at Portsmouth, which was nearing the end of a long refit and had been fitted out as the Flagship of the West Indies Fleet to be under the command of Admiral Sir William Tennant. I was to be the Warrant Telegraphist of H.M.S. Sheffield and for the West Indies Fleet -- an appointment many would have given their right arm for.

H. M. S. SHEFFIELD

My initial reaction to this appointment was not one of the greatest pleasure. I had been married for less than three years and spent just three months with my wife and was now off again for a further two and a half years. I remonstrated with the Admiralty about this but to no avail, only to be told how very fortunate I was to be given such an appointment and that in any case, in due course I might be able to have my wife in Bermuda. I disbelieved this as there was absolutely no movement of Navy wives and families accompanying their husbands anywhere in the world and in any event, even though it happened for officers before the war, it was only at the officer's personal expense, therefore only the wealthy could afford such luxuries. Looking back now, this appointment was not just one out of the hat; I had quite clearly been specially selected with my future career in mind. The commander of Sheffield was a Viscount Garmoyle, formerly the Hon. D.C. Cairns for whom I had served as a messenger in the Signal School in 1938. I believe in this lowly position, I did an efficient job for him and believe that it was at his request I was appointed to Sheffield under the direct eye of the Commander in Chief.

I joined Sheffield at Portsmouth in February, taking Thelma to Bognor where we took rooms in a rather nice house of a friend of my mother's. It worked out very well. We were comfortable and I was able to get home most evenings and weekends. At the same time I was able to see something of my parents and Thelma was for the very first time able to learn about becoming a housewife -- she learned fast, for I always had excellent meals prepared for me even though she had no previous experience.

There was very much work to be done on board, fitting out the various wireless offices, getting to know the equipment and training my staff. All quite formidable really but I can't remember having any worries over it. By the end of June, we were ready to sail for sea trials and subsequently to the West Indies. We sailed first to Portland, then on to Gibraltar, to Malta, back to Gibraltar and on to Azores. These preliminaries took two months and consisted of all the usual exercises: gunnery, torpedoes, anti-submarine, air attacks, etc. Needless to say the communication team was involved heavily in each of them. Meanwhile Thelma returned to her home in Liverpool, but did not take up work.

We reached Bermuda from the Azores on 30th August and had fifteen days to get to know the remainder of our fleet and for them to get to know us. It was necessary also to live closely with our colleagues ashore in Bermuda as well as the dockyard authorities. By the 15th September we had to sail as a fleet on our first post-war cruise to the West Indian Islands. The British people in these islands had been starved of contacts from home for many years and had seen nothing of the fleet that protected them. They were desperate for our visit -- and what a great welcome they gave us, everywhere we went. Sheffield called at Nassau, Jamaica, Trinidad, Granada, Barbados, and Antigua, each visit lasting three but no more than four days. It was one long round of parties and entertainment either on shore or aboard and always the climax was the "Beating of the Retreat" by the Royal Marines band at sunset, which brought tears to almost all ex-patriot eyes. The other ships of the fleet, all smaller vessels than Sheffield, paid their visits to the smaller islands so that there was never more than one Naval ship in any one port at the same time. The cruise was a great success but it was hard work and we were always glad of a couple of days rest at sea between islands. I had not known until now that living a high life was so exhausting!

We were back in Bermuda for my 28th birthday, October 15th, but for a very short stay as we had to represent Britain in New York for Trafalgar Day on the 21st October. We therefore sailed on the 19th, spent one glorious day in New York and returned to Bermuda on the 23rd for a rest and short refit. It was during this time that we collected Admiral Sir William Tennant, fresh out from England. Bermuda was as great a holiday as anywhere and now we had two months to enjoy it, which we did to the full. Nevertheless I was missing Thelma terribly and decided it was no use spending our lives apart. Whatever it may cost to get her to Bermuda and whatever it may cost us to live here, with no help from the Admiralty, she would have to come. I therefore obtained the necessary permission. There were a few other wives of Sheffield officers there, but in most cases only those of private means, whereas we would be required to exist solely on our pay.

Arrangements were made for Thelma to fly in early December. The plane was a converted war time bomber, with just one seat each side of a `gangway and a total capacity for about 20 passengers. It could not fly direct, having insufficient fuel, so would have to touch down in the Azores. I believe it took off from Blackbush airport in the morning and reached the Azores around 6pm. The runway was pretty rough, certainly not tarmacked and probably still bomb cratered. It was certainly a bumpy landing. When the aircraft stopped it was surrounded by crowds of local men, all peering through the windows, but none of the passengers were allowed to leave the plane I think Thelma had not a clue where she was or why she was there - very frightening. Later they took off again to arrive in Bermuda around 6am the following morning.

At my end I had problems. Bermuda is a series of some twenty or so islands connected to each other by road or bridge. However, the roads were nothing more than dusty tracks and no cars at all were allowed, except on the main island: Hamilton The dockyard was the furthest island to the East on Ireland Island and the airfield probably the furthest island to the West, about 20 miles. My only means of transport was bicycle and I had to be there by 6am. I was there, setting off before daylight at around 4am. I was able to watch the plane land and walk to it to help passengers alight. How glad I was to have Thelma with me once more.

I had arranged accommodation with a black Bermudan couple on Somerset Island. It was only one room, but accommodation was difficult to find on the dockyard side and I had to have an address before Thelma could be authorized to travel. I can't remember how we travelled from the airport to this shack -- possibly by taxi to Hamilton and then ferry to Somerset Island, but we made it and Thelma was able to rest after her arduous trip. This accommodation was most unsatisfactory for a number of reasons and we stayed but a short time before we were able to find rooms with another black Bermudan couple in a slightly larger house. Here at least we had two rooms: one to eat in and one to sleep.

I joined the Warrant Officer's Club on Somerset Island, a club for Warrant Officers of the Fleet, and Thelma became a member with me. We spent many happy evenings there as it was quite a lively club and made a number of friends among whom were Tess and Maurice. Maurice was an accountant in the dockyard and Tess also worked in his department. He offered Thelma a job in charge of wages for all dockyard workers, a task of no small measure long before the days of calculators and computers. All wages had to be calculated and dealt with manually, including of course overtime, stoppages, etc. Thelma was pleased to accept as it would give her something to do during the many months I would be away on cruises.

During this period between October and Christmas, Sheffield had a minor refit in the dockyard and on 4th January (1947) was ready to sail with the remainder of the Fleet for a South American tour -- the first by the Royal Navy since before the war. We called first at Jamaica for two days and then on to Colon, the entrance to the Panama Canal, through which we passed. We stopped at Balboa, the Pacific side for one day before proceeding to Callaro in Peru – the port for Lima. Here we spent five most wonderful days. As usual on the first evening, we were entertained by the local dignitaries and all of the British residents. The latter had not seen a British warship or the navy since 1939, as was the case with all the ports we were due to call at on this cruise. We had a wonderful trip arranged for us into the Andes, going up the perilous slopes by a single track railway. We went up to a small village known as Rio Blanco, bathed in cloud, river streams and waterfalls. The Hamas were friendly creatures but the terrain somewhat barren. The visit ended on the last evening with a grand cocktail party on board, attended by most of those we had met on the first evening and the "pièce de résistance": Beating the Retreat by the Royal Marines on the jetty at sunset, with the inevitable flood of tears and feeling of great pride that always accompanied this ceremony.

During this part of the voyage we crossed the equator going south, for which there was very much hilarity on board, commencing the day before we reached the line. Duly, on the morning of the day, quite early, the ship stopped and the Commander welcomed on board King Neptune, his entourage and court. The court was seated on the forecastle amidships on front of a huge ducking pool complete with ducking stools. The justice of the peace called the names of the offenders who were duly brought forward, often handcuffed and frequently prodded by King Neptune's three pronged spear. Without exception all were found guilty, duly greased from head to foot, head shaved, and tossed in the pool. All those who had never before crossed the line, of which I was one, were required to come forward, say their piece to King Neptune who ordered them to be shaved and thrown in. Thereafter they became a member of the "order of crossing the line". It was a really great day, thoroughly enjoyed by all.

We welcomed the three day break at sea on leaving Lima and moved on to Antofagasta in Chile for three days, arriving 22nd January. Antofagasta is the northernmost port of Chile and the capital of the State of Antofagasta. Here we had a repeat performance of the ceremonies at Callao but condensed into three days. Crowds lined the docks and jetties on the 25th to see and wave to us as we departed with ships sirens shrieking, etc. It was really touching to see all these British people, so cut off from their homeland, seeing us as their only link.

The next journey, to Valparaiso was quite short, just two days, hardly enough time to recover from the round of parties, but we needed all our strength for Valparaiso as it was going to be a six day visit. The city is quite large and widespread, not far from Santiago, capitol of Chile and home base for the Chilean Navy. Again we had the round of civic receptions, parties, night life and, additionally, entertainment of and by the Chilean Navy. The number of British people here was far greater than any of the ports visited to date, not surprising in view of the size of the place and its nearness to the capital from which many came.

Unfortunately we had no time to relax and recover from Valparaiso as our next visit was to Talcahuano, the port for Conception, only twenty four hours sailing. Here we spent another three days, similar to our visit to Antofagasta with little time for local sightseeing by ourselves. This was not to be the end of our Chilean visit as there was yet Puerto Monte to call at, for a further three days and after this, Punta Arenas on the southernmost tip of South America on our way through the Magellan Straights.

We spent three days in Punta Arenas -- a pretty bleak and generally cold place in mid-February, as it now was, despite being the height of their summer. It was important though because all down this Chilean coast were thousands of British ex-patriots and we hope we brought some hope and encouragement to their lives after six years of what had been a very bleak war for them. The celebrations never flagged and we gave and received as much as we had given in Valparaiso. By now we were quite well practiced though getting a little tired.

On 17th February we sailed around and away from South America, into the South Atlantic en-route for the Falkland Islands. It was only a two day trip but we were scheduled for six days in this small British Island, over which, in later years, there was to be a hard fought battle with Argentina. I think what I remember most from the Falklands are the masses of penguins -- a far larger population than that of the inhabitants. However, the cocktail parties were not for the penguins, nice as they were to see and amusing to watch. The Falklands seemed really cut off from the rest of the world and they treated us like long lost relations come to visit them. Generally all were poor, living very simple lives with little knowledge of what was happening in the rest of the world. Their only newspaper, The Falkland Times, was a double sheet measuring 8" x 6" (200mm x 150mm), produced on a typewriter and duplicated. They gave us a most wonderful reception and visit within their limited means and we gave them a small taste of civilization. Of all of the places we visited, it was this island that was so sorry to see us leave, but it had to be as we had much more work to do.

Our next call was to Montevideo, Uruguay for seven days, arriving there after three days' rest at sea, to get our breath back, which we were going to need on this visit. The Battle of the River Plate had been fought off Montevideo in the early days of the war, and the German battleship Graf Spee stunk here. But this was in the past and we were calling now to greet the very large numbers of British living there. What a welcome, surpassing all others that we had encountered and what a visit. From the Ambassador's reception on the first night it was entertainment every night so much so that there were three invitations for every one that could be met It became necessary to draw up a roster and detail officers which invitation they had to accept and this often meant more than one per day. The bright lights and night life was far greater than anything I had ever seen before and the city full of the most beautiful buildings to say nothing of the fabulous beaches. Here, in addition to the traditional "Beating of the Retreat" on our last night, the ship's company and Royal Marines carried out a "March Past" the Mayor led by the Royal Marine Band. It was a visit none of us ever wanted to end, but as usual it had to be for we were due in Buenos Aires, Argentina on 7th March. Being only just across the River Plate Estuary, this took no more than a few hours sailing time.

The schedule at Buenos Aires was five days and like Montevideo, it was five days of the most hectic lifestyle. All the hundreds of invitations were there as usual and the rosters for acceptance duly organized so that no one could opt out. There were rumblings from the Argentine Government about the Falklands belonging to them and not us; we had demonstrated our loyalty to the Falklanders and paid no attention to Argentine claims. In any case we were there to bolster the morale of the British residents, as well perhaps as to show our strength to the Argentines. Five days at Buenos Aires was as much as we wanted, in fact for many it would have been welcome if the cruise could end here, such hard work was it. Our next call was to be Santos –the port for San Paulo.

One of the events for which I was nominated was a visit to a stud-farm. I knew anything about horses, but I was about to learn. After the preliminaries of cocktails etc., we were taken to the stables and each allocated a horse. Certainly they were beautiful racehorses and I think I must have been given the pick of the bunch for no sooner was I on his back than he was raring to go. After a short trot and canter they let him have his head and off he shot like a bolt out of the blue. There was no way that I could stop him; my only concern was to stay on his back. I didn't know when he would stop or where he would go. Fortunately, one of the riding instructors caught up eventually and slowed him down. I was never so glad to get off anything as I was that horse.

Fortunately there was a three day break at sea on leaving Buenos Aires and this was extremely welcome giving us a little time to re-gather strength and arrive at Santos for a four day visit on 15th March. The performances were all exactly the same as for other ports on the cruise and after our four days we moved on to Rio de Janeiro, this time for five days. Another very great and welcoming city, equal to Montevideo or Buenos Aires. All of us were weary by this time - I hope it did not show. Anyway we most thoroughly enjoyed everything that was laid on for us.

Our next, and last, visit in South America was to Recife (Pernambuco) with three days of rest at sea before arriving on a visit of four days. It was all the same old routine for us and I hope we showed as much enthusiasm a we had on our visit to Callao, some three months earlier. One thing I am sure is certain, we were all looking forward to six days at sea after leaving Recife. It had been a most wonderful trip the whole of the way around South America, not just sailing from port to port but full of entertainment the whole way. Not a journey that has been done by very many and I was privileged to be in Sheffield and to participate.

From Recife we sailed back to Trinidad where we had been six months earlier. I think the white residents here were more than pleased to see us, but not particularly the Trinidadians. It was however a British Colony and necessarily received our attention. We stayed here just four days without all the jollifications we had received and given at the South American ports and a very welcome visit it was indeed. This visit was followed by a four day sea trip to Bermuda where we arrived, tired, but somewhat more experienced in social life on 15th April.

Sports played an extremely important part of life on Sheffield. At all ports of call the locals did all possible to provide facilities and produce formidable opposition. The activities included water polo, football, cricket, Rugby, hockey, boxing, and rifle shooting. My own contribution was to football where I played for the first eleven as a forward, plus some water polo and a little cricket, in neither of which could I excel. The highlight of the football team was the winning of the Bermuda Cup in which we beat a hefty team of Bermudans 3-2 after extra time. It was a great match, broadcasted and attended by a large crowd (more than 1000 from Sheffield and the dockyard) and we were pleased to be presented with medals by the Governor and chaired off the field by our supporters after the game. In Jamaica we played the Suffolk regiment and won 1-0. At Lima we played a club which had beaten Everton before the war -- we were well and truly beaten 5-0. At Antofagasta we played the Railway club and won 2-1, again at Valparaiso we won 5-2 and at Talcahuano we played the Chilean Navy winning 4-1. At Punta Arena we had a hard game before a huge crowd being unlucky in losing 1-2, whilst at Falkland Islands we drew with the Island team 1-1. At Montevideo, where the locals often got so excited they shot at the referee, we lost 4-6. Pity they did not shoot at him during this match. Both at Santos and Rio de Janeiro the opposition was far too strong and we lost 12-1 and 10-0 respectively whilst at Recife, our last game of this cruise, we won 6-0. The final tally was, played 13, won 8, drew 1, and lost 4, with 33 goals saved and 33 against. After each match the team was presented with a memento and I collected 3 flags, 1 plaque, 2 cups, and 3 medals.

During our absence, an important step had been taken by Admiralty in as much that official approval was given for the wives of any of the officers or men to join them if they so wished. This meant that an overseas allowance would be paid to us to cover the extra cost of living and that Thelma would have perhaps more company during the lengthy periods that I was away. Two other officers from the Warrants Officer's mess had arranged for their wives to come, and a number of others from the wardroom. It was lovely to see them all on the jetty awaiting our arrival on 15th April -- the excitement for those involved was enormous, needless to say. Thelma was among them. We were now to spend ten weeks in Bermuda and looking forward to every minute of it. We found out that a small one bedroom flat was being built at the rear of the cycle shop on Somerset Island and wasted no time in applying for it. We were lucky as the Bermudan owner agreed to

Under the banana trees in Bermuda

let it to us and were able to move from our somewhat crummy and cramped rooms. The flat was very small, one living room off the front door, one bedroom, a tiny kitchen and toilet with washbasin and shower.

Water was obtained only from what could be caught on the roof during the infrequent showers. This was filtered down through the building to a concrete basement where it was stored and pumped up for use by an electric pump. If the tank ran dry, water could be bought and delivered, but it was an expensive commodity. Electricity was laid on. We had a tiny garden at the rear, whose main feature was a banana tree. We were extremely happy in this first little home of our own Thelma got along famously with the other wives, particularly a Mrs. Turner, wife of the president of the Warrant Officer's mess and Pat Bridle, wife of the electrical warrant officer with whom she made a life-long friendship. She was happy with her somewhat responsible job in the dockyard and, having officially called on Sir William and Lady Tennant was invited to tea at Admiralty House. Looking back now, there was a motive for such invitation: it was to vet Thelma and establish if she was a suitable person to fit into wardroom life. If she was not, then any promotion prospects of mine would vanish. Clearly she passed with flying colours and indeed got along very well with Lady Tennant. Just as well that we were not aware of the implications at this time for I had not the faintest idea that I would soon be a specially selected officer. During this ten week period, Thelma became pregnant, but at this early stage the pregnancy had little effect on our lives apart from the usual symptoms experienced by mothers-to-be. We were, of course, absolutely thrilled with this development as we had both longed for a child of our own and although married almost four years now, had barely spent enough time together to do anything about it.

Eventually our day of departure arrived yet again, June 27th. It had been a most wonderful ten weeks of happiness and pleasure a full social life and everything that we could wish for. One of the more pleasant experiences was dinghy sailing, from the ship out and across the Sound towards Hamilton. The ship's Bos'n, an experienced sailor, would accompany us on these trips as I was not capable of handling even a dinghy in such circumstances. Sometimes it would blow up rough in a matter of minutes and on one occasion so rough that even our experienced skipper had some difficulty in getting the boat back. We arrived back at Sheffield, all thoroughly drenched to the skin and Thelma was given an officer's bathroom to bath and recover in -- much against Naval Tradition but she enjoyed getting in to perhaps the largest bath she has ever seen. Our next cruise was to be a little over three months, calling at the ports along the East Coast of Canada and the United States. This was bound to be hectic as not only would we have the civilians at each port to entertain and be entertained by, but also the Canadian and U.S. Navies. As with our South American cruise, this was the first post war visit by the Royal Navy.

Our first stop was at Halifax Nova Scotia, not unknown to me by any means. But it was a different Halifax that I was to see now, compared with that in the days of H.M.S. Vanoc and the war. It is the Eastern Port for the Canadian fleet and we were given a tremendous welcome here. Quite a long visit really, it lasted seven days before we moved further north to Dalhousie, New Brunswick in the Gulf of St. Lawrence -- two days sailing. Dalhousie is quite a small town, but nevertheless a port, and as each ship of the West Indies fleet was calling at a different port, quite a number could be covered. Four days here was sufficient for all the standard entertainment as on the South American cruise and we then moved across to St. John's Newfoundland, another two days sailing and of course quite well known to me from the convoy days of the war. Here again we spent seven full days. We left St. John's on 25th July and for the next two weeks cruised off the northern coast of Newfoundland, Labrador as far as Hudson Bay, exercising with the remaining ships of the fleet and calling at various small ports just for the day or sometimes the night. The waters in these ports are not inviting and tend to be cold, even in the summer. One part of the exercise, not scheduled, was my transference from Sheffield to a frigate whilst under-way at sea. A transmitter on one of the ships had failed; it could not be made to work, so the job was for me. The transfer took place by the two ships concerned steaming a parallel course, about 25 yards apart -- rather more difficult than it sounds. A line is fired from one ship to the other and a steel hawser pulled across to which is attached a running pulley. The hawser is attached to each ship but must readily extend or contract, to account for slight variations in the distance between ships, or rolling of either or both ships. Attached to the pulley is a steel wire with a foothold on to which I climbed and in this fashion, with a life line round my body, I was pulled across. Somewhat apprehensively, but safely I reached the other vessel and in due course sorted out the problems of the smaller boat and got their transmitter back into operation. I remained aboard thereafter until we anchored for the night whence I returned by ship's boat.

On 14th August, we entered the St. Lawrence River and sailed down to Quebec, a city of some size and importance. Here we spent a full week of great entertainment, reminiscent of the South American days and on the 22nd for a further full week at Montreal. At both of these cities we were given the full treatment and had a really wonderful time on top of the great interest of sailing down the St. Lawrence River. Unfortunately it all ended on 29th August when we sailed back up the St. Lawrence and on to Boston U.S.A and Connecticut. I had been here before, but this was a visit with a difference, having the U.S. Navy to deal with and the entertainment being somewhat lavish. We were here for six days during which I decided to take a few days leave to visit a distant relation of Fred Chilton, my colleague of Vanoc days and now my brother in law.

Thelma had decided that rather than stay in Bermuda on her own, she would join me for part of this cruise, using the money we had received in back-pay for our overseas allowance. She was by now three months pregnant and the only way to get to the States quickly was by flying boat from Bermuda to Baltimore. From there she would travel by train to Newhaven, Connecticut where our hosts lived and I would meet her there, going by train from Boston - about one hour's journey. Thelma's flight was not without incident. The flying boat flew low and the flight was extremely bumpy. It was about a six hour flight and, being pregnant she was taken violently sick and was laid out at full stretch on an improvised bed, provided with ice bags and the full attendance of a nurse. At Baltimore there was a question as to whether or not she should be taken to hospital, but when the flight was over, she fairly quickly recovered and was able to face the immigration and customs official for fingerprinting and third degree about her intentions in the United States. She then travelled by taxi to Baltimore railway station and eventually on to Newhaven -- another long journey by rail. Our hosts, Helen and Harry not only made us very comfortable but were extremely kind to us. We got along so well that Helen decided to accompany Thelma down to New York where she would be going next to meet the Sheffield on arrival. Meanwhile I returned to the ship at Boston for the sailing to New York.

It was just a twenty four hour trip to New York and Thelma and Helen had booked into a hotel for the three of us for the seven day visit. They were there to see the Sheffield arrive on the 8th Sept.

As expected, New York was the highlight of this cruise. A ticker tape welcome would be putting it mildly. Invitations came in abundance, ship open to visitors every day, cocktail parties on board and ashore. There were just not enough members of the ship's company to meet all obligations and certainly no free time for normal shore leave. The highlight of this visit was a grand ball, given by The Association of British Empire Societies under the patronage of the British General Consul. This ball was attended by the British Ambassador, the Ambassadors of Australia, Canada, New Zealand, and South Africa, the mayor of New York, all top Admirals of the U.S. Navy and every person of note in New York. Dancing was from 9pm to 2am, with an interlude for our Royal Marine Band to give a musical display and military pageant. This was really a great night. I had collected Thelma and Helen from their hotel at about 7pm in my full uniform splendour and arranged a taxi to take up to the ball. There was a demonstration outside of the Armoury in which the ball was being held. It seems there was an anti-British feeling from the Jewish population of New York, objecting to the British stand against Jews returning to the Middle East to establish their own country. The situation around our taxi became quite ugly. Thelma wanted me to remove my Naval cap and sneak in. Perhaps foolishly, I refused, alighted from the taxi and escorted the ladies inside with no harm done. The incident was soon forgotten, once inside. Our visit to New York lasted a full seven days -- only the fittest survived, but twenty four hours at sea on our way to Philadelphia was enough for most of us to recover.

Thelma and Helen travelled by rail down to Philadelphia. In fact, Helen was due to return to her husband from New York, but she was enjoying herself so much and had made a friend of one of my colleagues from the Warrant Officer's mess, so she telephoned her husband and arranged to stay a further week. Philadelphia was a repeat of New York to a large extent although on a smaller scale and rather more pleasant. Here, the British community on learning that Thelma was pregnant, gave us a gift of a baby Layette consisting of everything we would need, they were very kind. Here also we purchased the most gorgeous pram imaginable from the top store. It was like a Royal Carriage, huge, comfortable, well sprung, large wheels and beautifully finished in dark grey. It was magnificent. I have no idea how we took it away, presumable it was carefully packed and crated and delivered to Sheffield.

From Philadelphia, after six days, we said our farewells to Helen and Thelma embarked on her flying boat trip back to Bermuda, whilst Sheffield sailed on to Norfolk, Virginia the main Naval Base of the U.S. Navy and only one day's sailing. The five days at Norfolk were not particularly exciting and were concerned mainly with entertainment by and of the U.S. Navy, so that when we left on 28th September we were more than a little glad of the four days at sea, back to Bermuda, and back, thankfully, to Thelma.

Within a few days of our return to Bermuda, a signal was received from the Admiralty stating that I had been selected for direct promotion to Lieutenant and was required to return to the United Kingdom immediately for nine months of intensive training in all aspects of a Lieutenant's duties. This was quite an unexpected departure and one that had not particularly ever occurred to me. I was of course thrilled in the extreme. Direct promotion from Warrant Rank was a relatively recent innovation. Previously it had only been possible to become a Wardroom Officer through Dartmouth. Now, here was I about to join them with only fifteen others from the whole of the Royal Navy and no others from the West Indies Fleet. I was most certainly honoured. Looking back, pieces of the jigsaw fall into place and revolve around Earl Cairns, who I believe selected me for the Fleet Warrant Telegraphist and then put through a recommendation to Admiral Sir William Tennant who passed it on to the Admiralty, remembering that Lady Tennant had already vetted Thelma and approved. I had spent just twenty months in Sheffield, twenty very happy months.

Now other problems arose. I had to return to the U.K. but Thelma, being almost six months pregnant, was not allowed to fly and sea passages were almost unavailable. In any case she could not travel unaccompanied. It seemed at one stage that I might have to return and leave her in Bermuda. Eventually, Thelma's boss in the dockyard and his wife Tess, friends of ours, came to the rescue. He discovered that there was a small merchant vessel leaving Bermuda in late October, going on to the West Indian Islands and eventually back to Avonmouth with a cargo of bananas. Steps were quickly taken to obtain a passage for us. It was not a ship normally to carry more than around six passengers but our case was urgent and we obtained a first class double berth. And so, after a round of farewell parties including cocktails and lunch with Admiral Sir William Tennant, we joined S.S. Bayano in Bermuda on 31st October and sailed that day for the West Indies.

S.S. Bayano

Before my departure in Bayano, another somewhat frightening experience occurred in Bermuda. A hurricane had been tracked, heading for Bermuda which was likely to hit the island. Accordingly, Sheffield put to sea to ride out the storm as it would have been much too dangerous to stay alongside in harbour. I had to leave Thelma in our tiny bungalow to fend for herself, although heavily pregnant. We had a considerably rough time at sea when the hurricane hit, but although it was uncomfortable, we were safe - unlike those poor people left on the island where much damage was done. Thelma was completely confined to the bungalow and chose not so much as to open a door. Our banana tree was up-rooted and blown away and she was terrified, being alone. In the middle of the storm she had a caller – it was an American woman, from a small home lying back to back with ours. She had risked her neck to call and see if Thelma was all right, or if there was any food she could share with her. Although we did not know this person, it was a most courageous and humanitarian act on her behalf. After four days, the hurricane passed, we returned to harbour and the work of clearing up the devastation began.

The Bayano was a fairly slow ship, quite old, and had been on the West Indies banana run for many years. We had a comfortable cabin, dined with the Captain and officers of the ship and had little to do all day, except watch the flying fish or porpoises travelling with the ship. Down at Jamaica, we called first at Kingston, known reasonably well to me by now and Thelma and I explored the island by taxi. Then we sailed all around the northern-most parts of Jamaica. Here there were no ports, just seaside villages and the ship had to anchor outside in most cases. Imagine Thelma's horror when she spotted a fleet of canoe type boats, manned by local men, pulling their boats towards the ship. She was sure we were about to be attacked with spears and the like. In fact these were boats bringing out the bananas for loading. There was another frightening sight at one of the places where the ship was able to get alongside a jetty. A man with a huge sabre like knife stood at the head of the gangway. Running up the gangway, with a huge branch of bananas on each back, came black men and women. As they passed the man with the chopper he would bring it down with a swipe, just missing their heads but chopping off a stalk from the branch. The loaders were paid half penny for each stalk. I don't know what they were paid for a head - we failed to see one disappear. I think we both found this experience around Jamaica quite fascinating. Eventually when the ship's holds had been filled with bananas we were ready to sail with our cargo and wasted no time in doing so. I think the journey home, at little more than six knots, was to take us three weeks, but we were comfortably installed on board so all was well. Somewhere in mid Atlantic we ran into a gale causing the boat to roll, pitch and toss. Thelma took to her bunk as I believe did most other passengers, but I tucked her in securely so that she would not roll out. She did not like it, but would have to ride the storm. The sea was heavy enough to smash down a bridge stanchion and I saw no one in the dining room other than a couple of officers for two days. Rather foolishly I decided to take a bath whilst this storm was raging. Unfortunately instead of the bath being installed fore and aft it was installed athawtships, consequently when the ship rolled, all the water went flooding over the end of the bath and out into the corridor. At the cries of "What the B --- fool is having a bath". I hopped out quickly and drained the water away, whilst the steward had to mop up the overflow. On one occasion during the voyage, Thelma called the ship's doctor to check up on the unborn baby. I think he knew very little about such things really, but assured us all was well.

The wind dropped, the sea calmed and we rolled merrily on our way until one morning when we came on to deck huge nets of bananas were being lifted from the hold, hoisted overboard and dumped in the sea. Behind us, for miles, all we could see was a trail of floating banana stalks. It appears that in one hold, a stalk of over ripe bananas gave off a rather nasty gas. It was imperative to dispose of them at sea as they would have been of little use by the time we reached port. This operation went on for two days and was heart-breaking, bearing in mind that bananas had not been seen in England since before the war -- over six years since. On we sailed, heading for Avonmouth, eventually arriving without further incident on 21st November 1947. It was a most convenient time to arrive and allowed me leave, and Christmas at home before joining H.M.S. Excellent at Portsmouth for my Lieutenants' course. Accordingly we went to Thelma's home in Liverpool.

LIEUTENANT'S COURSE

During this six week period, it was necessary to find accommodation for ourselves near Portsmouth and to arrange a nursing home for Thelma to have our first baby. We were perhaps fortunate to find a small secluded bungalow in Southsea which was adequate for our needs and I looked into a nursing home for Thelma in Southsea. We moved there immediately after Christmas and I started my courses at the gunnery school (H.M.S. Excellent) on 5th January.

These courses, which were to take ten months, included gunnery, torpedoes, ASDICs, communications, RADAR, navigation, seamanship, and general duties as well as behaviour of wardroom officers. Although attached to H.M.S. Excellent, it did mean spending time at other specialist establishments, all of which centred around Portsmouth and of spending a good deal of time at sea with the training squadron, mainly at Portland. I entered with enthusiasm and excitement, thoroughly enjoyed the whole period and kept at or among the top of the group in most subjects. Navigation was a particular favourite of mine, being mathematically oriented. Not so gunnery or torpedo work. Communications was just a holiday for me. Anyway I passed very successfully and was duly promoted to Lieutenant with a seniority back dated to 1945.

Thelma duly entered the nursing home on 1st February, 1948 and produced the most beautiful baby on 2nd with no complications. It is every parent's belief that their baby is the loveliest of all babies, but in this case it was true. Christine, as we were to christen her, was the most beautiful child, "born with a tan as though straight from Bermuda". She has loved the sun ever since. Thelma was in the nursing home for two full weeks and I was able to visit every day. Back at home, routines had to be altered somewhat, but we adapted and the smart super-pram from America was brought into use. Apart from having a lovely baby, the pram was the centre of attention. Wherever Thelma pushed it, people turned round to look again, thinking it was Royalty I am sure. If it was left outside a shop, as was possible in those days, there would be people gathered around it when Thelma returned, trying to discover the manufacturer.

During the period I had the usual two weeks leave at Easter and in the summer, at which times we travelled by train to Thelma's home. It was during our first Easter Holiday (28th March, 1948) that we had Christine christened at All Saints Church, Stoneycroft, with all the due pomp and ceremony and her mother laid on an excellent party for all.

H.M.S. ZODIAC

On promotion to Lieutenant, I was appointed to H.M.S. Zodiac of the Portland flotilla, my duties on board being those of correspondence officer and Captain's secretary, normally undertaken by a sub-Lieutenant. Additionally of course, there were the normal watch-keeping duties as officer of the watch and, in harbour, officer of the day. We belonged to the training flotilla and so spent much time on exercises with other ships and made visits to Torquay, Londonderry, and Douglas, Isle of Man, but most of our time was spent at Portland.

We relinquished our bungalow at Southsea and took a small terraced house in Weymouth so that I could see as much of Thelma and Christine as possible. However, whilst on my Lieutenant's courses, Thelma became pregnant again and before leaving Portsmouth our second little girl was born, this time, because of certain complications, at St. Mary's Hospital in Portsmouth in November 1949. It was not a happy confinement. Thelma did not like the hospital nor get on well with the staff -- somewhat different to the nursing home. Nevertheless the baby, Julia as we subsequently christened her, was another beautiful baby, quite different from Christine. She was fair and blue eyed and had a lovely quiet nature. Zodiac was at Portsmouth during this time and so again, I was able to visit them every day. There was plenty of room in our large pram for both of them and I was a very proud father of two lovely daughters.

So we took up our house in Weymouth with two babies, but my commanding officer took a dim view of the situation. Here was I, a new Lieutenant basically still under training, but shooting off ashore to my family at every opportunity. I was always ready to be stepping ashore over the gangway at 4pm to be with my family and back at 8am next morning. He felt that my interest was only to be at home and never mind the service. At the same time, in no way did I neglect my duties on board and within six months, the Captain had ceased to treat me with contempt and gave me every respect. His work was done and his parting reference for me said I had worked entirely to his satisfaction, "a most reliable and capable officer with a keen sense of duty and responsibility".

One other small incident occurred during this period, at Christmas 1949 whilst Thelma was still in our bungalow at Southsea. I elected to take second leave from 28th Dec. and so be one of the duty-watch for Christmas. However I was not on duty for Christmas day, so booked up in a Naval hotel in Weymouth for Thelma and the babies so that I could be with them. The hotel management were so honoured by this that they asked me to make a speech I had never spoken in public before, but had to agree and no doubt muttered a few appropriate words, but I was scared to death!

During our stay at Weymouth our house was large enough to accommodate others so that Thelma's parents were able to have a holiday with us which they greatly enjoyed and my own parents were able to come down and visit us.

In March 1950, Zodiac returned to Portsmouth for a month. With two children now, it seemed appropriate that we should have a home of our own, preferably not too far from Portsmouth. After a short search we found a bungalow that was suitable, just outside Emsworth and so purchased it for a little under £2,000. It suited our needs, we were very happy there and Thelma quickly settled in making many friends from the local people. We left our rented house in Weymouth and settled into our own home. It soon became obvious that I needed a car, to travel from Emsworth to Portsmouth and take the family about when I was home and so I purchased a 1934 Morris which got us around and in which we had many adventures. I was able to drive, having learned on service vehicles when I was in the port party in Bombay and Italy, so I had no great problem in passing the driving test, after a little help from a driving school. This car, by modern standards would have to be seen to be believed. It would seat 4 just, it had no boot, the spare wheel was strapped on the back and there was a small folding iron rack behind the spare wheel, for cases. We put a roof rack on top to take extra luggage when required. Its normal speed was 30 MPH and top speed 40-45. Amazingly enough we used it to travel from Emsworth to Liverpool although we always had an overnight stop at Thelma's relations in Birmingham. All roads in those days were little more than lanes and there were no sign posts, these having been removed during the war to confuse the enemy. Getting up hills was a problem and if it was at all steep, my passengers (usually only Thelma) had to get out and push whilst I gave the engine full power. When going on a journey we obtained from the Automobile Association an itinerary which would read "proceed to the George & Dragon, then turn left. After one mile turn right, by the water works" etc., etc. Thelma had to be the navigator. On one occasion whilst travelling to Liverpool we had a puncture in the rear wheel. Luggage was removed from the back and placed by the roadside. A jack was found inside the car and I told Thelma and the children to stay put whilst I changed the wheel. Needless to say when I removed the punctured wheel the jack collapsed and I was left with the axle on the ground. Now what! All out except baby Julia in the carry cot on the back seat -- but there was nothing I could do except walk to find the nearest garage and as it was late in the day and we were in the middle of country quite uninhabited. Very fortunately, two farm workers came along on a tractor and stopped to help.

The two of them just lifted the back of the car whilst I slipped on the spare wheel and we were ready to go again. How simple it all seemed and how grateful was I to those two farm workers.

At the end of June 1950, whilst in Portsmouth, I received my next appointment: to H.M.S. Constance, a fairly modern destroyer of the Far Eastern Fleet. I was to join a troop ship — Empire Trooper, for passage at Southampton on 1st of August. I duly left Zodiac for some leave before embarkation and to make arrangements for Thelma during my absence; I had one month.

H.M.S. CONSTANCE

Neither Thelma nor I relished the thought of another two and a half year separation. After some discussion, it was decided that if possible, Thelma and the children would come to Hong Kong where the eighth destroyer flotilla was based and we could continue our family life there. A trip to the Admiralty in London was therefore arranged to investigate the possibility. We set off from Emsworth in our little Morris saloon, had an uneventful journey to London and parked alongside Green Park whilst I went into the Admiralty and the children played in the park. Yes, Thelma and the children could come to Hong Kong but it was necessary for me to go first and find suitable accommodation before passage could be granted. This was good news. After a pleasant day in the park we returned home to make the next arrangements. Quite clearly it would be necessary to let our bungalow and rather than give Thelma the worry of this decided we would find furnished accommodation reasonably close to her parents where she could live until called. Accordingly we found a ground floor flat of a large house in Wallasey, close to the sea which would suit Thelma's needs for what we hoped would be a few weeks and placed our bungalow in the hands of an estate agent who had no difficulty in finding a tenant. We moved up to Wallasey and settled in during the latter half of July.

I left on the 31st July, went to Southampton and joined Empire Trooper, confident in the knowledge that my family would be joining me in Hong Kong, probably by Christmas. We sailed on the 2nd August and made our way down to Port Said by the 12th.

Our stop was brief as we sailed again the same day, down though the Suez Canal, Red Sea, Arabian Sea and on to Aden by the 18th. Here we spent 24 hours and moved on to Colombo (Sri Lanka or Ceylon), in and out the same day and next stop Singapore where Constance was just completing a refit and due to return to Hong Kong.

I was to be the navigator of this fine ship, a prospect which thrilled me to the marrow but held no fears. The navigator is perhaps the most important man aboard, certainly at sea. The captain relies on him implicitly for the safety of his ship at all times. I had 48 hours to take over from the previous navigator who was now returning to the U.K. We then had two weeks of working up exercises off Singapore, to ensure that all was well with all equipment after the refit and that the crew were brought back to full efficiency. This period of three weeks in Singapore was exceptionally enjoyable. The officers knew the places, clubs and people, having been there over two months and I was quickly accepted into the fold. They were a really great wardroom, such a happy ship no doubt due to the 1st Lieutenant, James Long, one of the nicest persons I have ever met. James had recently married his wife in Hong Kong so the situation looked good. On 20th September we left Singapore for Hong Kong, a four day trip and my first attempt to navigate it to the right place.

There are two kinds of navigation, coastal and ocean. Coastal navigation requires close attention and full concentration. One is always within sight of the shore with its lighthouses and other navigational marks from which bearings can be taken to establish the ships exact position at any time. RADAR also plays a major part in coastal navigation. RADAR navigation was a relatively new concept known as "blind navigation", carried out by taking RADAR bearings of points of land in conjunction with depths from the echo sounder. As the RADAR gave both bearings and distance it could be first class if used with care, ensuring that the RADAR was accurately calibrated for ranges and bearings. Being an ex-warrant telegraphist I was completely convinced of this method and used it extensively and successfully in poor visibility or at night. Others were not so convinced and used it only in emergency, treating the results with scepticism. Ocean navigation, on the other hand, offers no aids other than the sun, moon and stars. The sun and moon are of little use owing to their brightness, their size and their rapid movement. Stars however, are very accurate if correctly identified and the precise angle and time accurately measured. The work cannot be done in darkness when stars are best visible, nor in day light when they cannot be seen. A fix is therefore taken just as dawn is breaking and again at dusk. One might say that if the ship is steered a certain course at a certain speed, you will always know where she is. This is not so, as wind and tide have their effect on the course and the sea conditions plus tide on the speed of the ship. A "fix" is a calculation using approximately six stars (or planets) by taking their angle with a sextant at a very precise time down to the second and computing a bearing. This is a lengthy and complicated affair which would use workings from top to bottom of an A4 sheet. When all bearings are obtained they are plotted on to a chart and where they cross is the position of the ship. It would be rare for all six to cross in one place but five probably will - the sixth may well have been an error in identification of the star.

I am sorry about this brief navigational lesson but it is impossible to appreciate the responsibility of a navigator's job unless a little is known about it. The journey from Singapore to Hong Kong can be plotted in a straight line across the South China Sea, running close to the shore alongside Vietnam (about half way). The captain would inspect my dead reckoning course and approve it, or otherwise, then it was up to me to keep the ship, as far as possible, on or close to it. On a four day trip, with

Vietnam showing up about half way, I would probably only need to take fixes (sights) on two days. Whatever, we safely reached Hong Kong on the 24th September, at the correct time and my first journey was over.

At about this time, trouble flared up in Korea between the North and South. The communist backed north was attempting to impose its will on the democratic south. The north had the advantage of Chinese troops to assist them and the south, no one except the free world. The United Nations was called upon to help. Troops were sent from U.N. members, mainly British and American whilst warships of all U.N. nations were sent to help. The thirty eighth parallel was designated the border between north and south and any intrusion over this line would result in heavy fighting. Without question, the eighth destroyer flotilla was the prime selection for the British Naval force. But what of Thelma and her journey to Hong Kong now, as we were likely to spend little time in Hong Kong?

I consulted my captain who at that stage said I should do what I thought best but he strongly advised against any such move. The question was settled within a few days when the Admiralty signalled that all naval passages to Hong Kong were suspended for the duration of the Korean war and that, disappointing as it was, settled the matter.

Needless to say, Thelma was distraught. She had given up her small home which she loved, moved to a place in which she really did not want to live and on top of that, was not going to see me for some time We decided that for the time being she should stay put with the hopes that this war would die out in a few months. In fact it went on for the next four years!

Our stay in Hong Kong was necessarily brief, just one week before we had to set sail for Korea. This was enough time however for me to enjoy a few of the sights and a little of the excitement that this great colony offered.

Hong Kong is a city like no other, full of hustle and bustle, very much over-crowded and offering services that would be found nowhere else in the world. For instance a "made to measure" suit could be ordered in the morning when all measurements would be taken and be ready to wear, fitting like a glove by the evening. My wardroom colleagues, who had been with

Hong Kong 1951

Constance for some time, knew Hong Kong well as the ship had spent much time there in the past. I had plenty of excellent company to show me around, keep me on the straight and narrow and teach me those places to which I should or should not go. I was lucky to have this expert knowledge to guide me for Hong Kong could be an equally dangerous place for those wandering alone.

On the second of October we sailed for Sasebo (Japan) to begin our Korean patrol. Sasebo was to be the base from which United Nations ships operated. It was situated just across the Korean Straights almost opposite Pusan and an excellent place from which to patrol the coast of Korea. Sasebo was a small Japanese naval port of very little consequence until now and offering few facilities in the way of recreation or amusement. Naturally, it was very Japanese, a culture so different from and alien to our own and it was more than a little difficult to accept as friendly, these people who had so cruelly treated our own not many years before. To most of us the relationship was strained and we would have little to do with them. However my second navigational trip was successful and we arrived at the right place at the right time without incident.

Our stay in Sasebo was very brief, just sufficient for us to size up the operation and position, get our orders, and sail on patrol. The first patrol was between Inchon (port for Seoul, capital of Korea) and Chinnampo, just

On the bridge H.M.S. Constance

south of Pyongyang, where fierce fighting was taking place between North Koreans backed by communist China and the South Koreans. Our job was to prevent any form of landing by the North Koreans which might cut off South Korean troops. This patrol lasted two weeks and it was then back to Sasebo, again for only three days, when, for some reason that I do not remember, we returned to Hong Kong and spent another delightful week. On the 1st December we went back again to Sasebo and immediately went on patrol until after Christmas. Then we were given a special treat and sent to Kure, Southern Japan for a week. Kure was a somewhat larger and rather more sophisticated port where we were able to see much more of the real life of the Japanese. We had a number of social invitations, none very much to our liking. Sitting cross legged, bare footed on the floor, eating raw fish was not much to my taste but one of those things which unfortunately had to be done. If nothing else it was a good rest which happened again for a week during February 1951.

Meanwhile we operated on Korean patrol which although for the most part uneventful, was still most unpleasant. The icy cold at this time of year was something none of us had previously experienced, only those unfortunate enough to have participated in Arctic convoys for Russia during the war could have known worse. It was impossible to keep warm whilst on watch up on the open bridge in spite of wearing all the clothes than we could possibly wear. During the daytime, the monotony would often be broken by a bombardment of enemy troops on shore. I have no idea whether any of our fire was effective, we had no one spotting for us, nor can I remember any retaliation although I have vague recollection of a bombing attack on one occasion. No damage done and no one killed.

Later in February we were rewarded by a visit to Yokosuka, the port for Yokohama on the west coast of Japan. It was short visit of three days allowing little time to see or do much and, in any case, after a couple of weeks of patrol, peace and rest was required. From 19th February it was back on patrol until 5th March when it became necessary to return to Hong Kong for an interim refit. Now we really could relax as we were to be in dockyard hands for nine weeks. It was during this time that I really got to know and enjoy Hong Kong and became saddened as the day approached for our return to Korea on 14th May 1951.

And so these seemingly endless patrols continued, up and down the west coast of Korea. On average, we had one day's rest for refuelling and re-victualing in Sasebo and two to three weeks on patrol. In July it was time to return to Hong Kong to pay off and re-commission the ship. At this time, it was customary for a ship to commission at its home port in the U.K. then sail, spend two and a half years on a foreign station and return to the U.K. to pay off and re-commission. It now became impossible to return ships all the way from China to the U.K. and the relief crew had to be sent by sea to join their ship on station. In July 1951 our Captain, a Commander A.M. Seale was relieved by Commander Lyle, the first being a highly competent seaman and the latter from the Fleet Air Arm who would need to and did place more reliance on the remaining officers. I was not due to be relieved in the re-commissioning having at that time only served one year of my commission, so I remained, with the new ship's company. Now came all the trials and tribulations of working the ship up to efficiency and three months was spent at Hong Kong to this end. The new crew had to get to know their ship, get to know each other, learn to operate their equipment, guns, torpedoes, depth charges, echo sounding, radar etc. and most of all they had to learn to work together as an efficient team. Three months was not a long time for this, it meant constant and persistent exercises day and night, boring at times but nevertheless essential. By November we were a fit and ready fighting unit and sailed back to Sasebo and the usual patrols so familiar to me by now but new to most of the remainder. Navigation wise, the trip from Hong Kong to Sasebo had become so familiar I could almost do it with my eyes shut and felt quite experienced.

In December, we covered the Choda Sokto Islands for three weeks and constantly during the first part of 1952 operated off Yang Do Island, patrolling at night, sinking Junks and capturing prisoners – North Koreans attempting to infiltrate South Korea. On the 24th, 25th and 3lst May we sank four junks, taking eighteen prisoners, all by blind navigation and were officially congratulated by the task force commander.

About this time, the United Nations Korean medal was awarded to all of those who had taken part in this war and the British Government issued its own Korean Medal to all of those involved, giving me two more to add to my collection. Presumably, awards were also made to the former ships company and recommended by Captain Seale, on paying off. I was again "mentioned in dispatches", the oak leaves for this mention to be worn on my British Korean medal. I don't know for what reason I received this award, except perhaps for devotion to duty - certainly I had carried out no acts of bravery.

Patrols continued throughout the winter of 1951 – 52 with the occasional visit to Kure but mostly to Sasebo for very brief periods of rest. It went on and on, monotonous and boring for the most part. Meanwhile, at home, Thelma had struggled on alone with the two babies all this time, very unhappy at her situation and with her accommodation. She wrote to me frequently as I did to her, seldom a day past that we did not write to each other – it was all we had between us and each time we returned to Sasebo I could not get to the mail to receive her letters quickly enough. In early summer 1952 she just could not stand living, isolated, in Wallasey any longer and made arrangements to return to our very own little bungalow in Emsworth pending my return due later in the year. She was much happier when she moved back to the South, renewing all the friendships she had made when living there earlier. Now all she had to do was to prepare and wait for my return.

On the night of the 9th June whilst on patrol off Yang Do, the captain decided to anchor for the night, visibility being poor. This was completely against his instructions but we anchored to the north of Yang Do in direct line of fire from the enemy battery on the mainland at four thousand yards. Instructions were left for the officer of the morning watch (the ship's 1st Lieutenant) to call the Captain at first light which he did. The Captain decided to move the ship to the south of Yang Do to be screened from enemy guns. He decided to make this move with the 1st Lieutenant and not to call me as, in his view, I had just completed one long and tiring patrol and my presence was unnecessary. Visibility was poor, so the 1st Lieutenant attempted to navigate the ship blind, having seen me do this so often. Without going into detail, within twenty minutes the ship was run well and truly onto the rocky bottom South of Yang Do. The first I knew of this was when I felt the bumps, ship juddering, and engines going full astern. Severe damage was caused to the propellers and the ASDIC dome was wiped clean away.

H.M.S. Constance damage to propeller

The ship was next ordered to Kure at very slow speed of course, where a board of enquiry was held at which I was to be a witness. The outcome of this was that both the Captain and 1st Lieutenant were to be court martialled in Singapore. The Captain was subsequently dismissed his ship and sent home whilst the 1st Lieutenant was severely reprimanded. Neither of these officers made any further progress in the Royal Navy.

It was in July 1952 that I received news of my relief being sent from the U.K. so that I could return home and in early August a Lieutenant Oliver Wright arrived. At that time the ship had gone down to Hong Kong and thence onto Singapore where it became necessary to enter dry dock for repairs necessitated by the accident of Commander Lyle's earlier in the year for which he was to be Court Martialled. Fortunately it was not necessary for me to remain behind as a witness for the Court Martial as I had been off duty and asleep at the time.

By the 9th August, I had completed the turn over and was fully relieved so that I could begin my journey home. It was to be by RAF transport plane and so I made my way to Changi Airport. The plane was a converted bomber, from the war, which had been stripped inside and makeshift seats arranged along the floor. Not very comfortable but who cared when we were on our way home after more than two years absence. The range of the aircraft was not great by modem standards. Our first hop was to Colombo where it was necessary to refuel, then to Aden, Alexandria, Malta and finally home. We only flew during daylight hours, remaining at each base over-night so that the journey took almost a week. However, we arrived at Brize-Norton safely and together with my bags and baggage caught a train to get me to Emsworth, via London.

On arrival at Emsworth in the early evening, there was Thelma with Christine and Julia waiting for me on the platform. It is impossible to describe the feeling of a reunion such as this after a two year absence. It was just wonderful. Thelma had not changed at all, still the beautiful young girl that I had left behind. Christine was a lovely little child of four and a half and Julia changed from a baby of six months to a lovely little toddler, almost three. Christine could well remember me, but to Julia I was just some man coming to intrude into their happy little lives. It must have been very difficult for her to accept. Thelma had purchased a lovely little car, no bigger than our first but comfortable enough to accommodate the four of us. It was an Austin Ruby Saloon of 1936 vintage but smart and sleek looking for that time. She had asked our next door neighbour to drive it to the station to meet me.

So now it was back home to our little bungalow in Southbourne and for an extensive leave during which time we were able to get to know each other again. My leave was spent between Southbourne and Liverpool with

The1ma's parents and the occasional visit to my own parents at Bognor. Whilst at Liverpool for Christmas 1952 when I had begun to think that the admiralty had forgotten about me, I received my next appointment, it was to be in command of a motor minesweeper MMS 1681.

IN COMMAND

MMS 1681 was part of the 51st Mine Sweeping Flotilla operating in the Firth of Forth and based at Port Edgar not far nom Rosyth. These MMSs were converted small ships which had been used pre-war as tenders to the large battleships. They used to sail with the fleet to the various ports where they were used for many duties by their parent ship, not least of which was taking hundreds of liberty men ashore. They were quite seaworthy but somewhat uncomfortable on which to live. The duty of this particular squadron was a new concept: that of mine hunting as opposed to mine sweeping. The object was, with the new technology, to hunt mines by sonar transmission and when discovered, to detonate them. This method had become essential in view of the magnetic mines moored beneath the surface and which would blow up ships passing over them before they could be swept. So I took command on the 26th January 1953.

MMS 1681

As this was likely to be another two year appointment, there was no way I was going to leave my family on the South Coast whilst I spent my time in Scotland. My first action therefore was to find suitable accommodation within striking distance of Rosyth. I found, eventually, a first floor flat in a large house, facing the Firth of Forth at the town of Burntisland, about fifteen miles along the coast. It was not the best but suited our needs. There was an extensive green opposite the house which led down to the seashore, through an arch, under the coastal railway. We moved in, late January, having driven our little car all the way via stops at Birmingham and Liverpool. Our own bungalow in Southbourne was once again let.

My new command had only one other officer on board, the 1st Lieutenant who, in this case, was an RNR officer who came from Newcastle on Tyne. The small crew consisted of around twenty men including, engine room staff, communications, and a wardroom steward. We would sail on exercises daily from Port Edgar under the Firth of Forth Bridge into the wider estuary where we would practice hour after hour, the technique of pinpointing mines. Seldom if ever were we required to stay at sea overnight, which was just as well as the exercises became very boring and at least I was able to get back to my family for the night.

An unfortunate incident occurred during my time with MMS1681. As Captain I was responsible for everything on board which included a welfare fund, a sum of money not great but kept locked in the ships safe to which only I had a key. When going on leave this key was turned over to the 1st Lieutenant, the cash having been checked against the accounts book. Whilst on Easter leave 1953 this routine was observed. On my return and checking off the money I found some was missing. As the 1st Lieutenant was the only one with the key I asked where the missing money was - he denied all knowledge or responsibility for it. The sum missing was minimal – perhaps £20 - but there was no way I could accept this even if it had been £1. The 1st Lieutenant could not give a satisfactory explanation, and continued with his denials that he had taken it or even borrowed it. I had no alternative but to report the matter to the Commander of the base. The officer was subsequently court martialled found guilty of theft and relieved of his position, in fact I think he was dismissed from the Royal Navy. I was glad to lose him, he had been a confidence trickster of the first order, always professing and boasting of his wealth, when in fact he had nothing and attempted to live by his wits. I'm afraid in this instance it failed to work.

Shortly before taking over MMS1681 Thelma had again become pregnant and our third baby was to be expected in August. We had to consider whether the flat in Burntisland would be suitable in which to bring another baby. We thought it would be. Soon after arrival in Burntisland, Christine started school. In Scotland, school was school right from the very first day. Fortunately Christine was bright and coped very well with this difficult work and in no time at all she was reading, writing and doing sums. Rather worse was poor Julia, she became ill and the doctor, when called, diagnosed pneumonia She was rushed into hospital at Kirkaldy, a little further along the coast. In fact she had double pneumonia and was very seriously ill, made worse by the fact that, at the age of three and a half, she was snatched from her home and family to be looked after quite impersonally by nurses and hospital staff. Thelma was distraught. She pleaded and fought in vain to be allowed to be in the hospital with Julia but NO, NO, NO! The Scottish theory was that it would be more upsetting for the child to have her mother in attendance than not. Quite unbelievable! Thelma was allowed the official visiting hours only Wednesday afternoons from three to four and Sunday afternoons from two to four. How very cruel. Slowly, but very slowly, Julia began to get better until eventually, after about six weeks she was allowed back home again. Meanwhile we were keeping our eyes open for more suitable accommodation and in mid-1953 were fortunate enough to find a small bungalow in its own grounds in Kirkaldy. We moved and were very happy and comfortable there. All this time Thelma's pregnancy was proceeding normally with no problems. On August 9th, feeling that the baby was due, she went to Kirkaldy Maternity Hospital. Here she relaxed with a good book until in the early hours of the 10th the nurse came to look at her and immediately panicked - the baby was due any second. The nurse said "Hold it, don't have it yet until the doctor arrives." He arrived in a short space of time and all was well, apparently the doctor gets no payment unless he is present at the birth - at least that was so in Scotland at that time. And so Karen, our third daughter, came into the world 10th August 1953.

During this summer, my mother's health, which had never been good, deteriorated somewhat rapidly commencing with the fact that she was unable to swallow. She was admitted to hospital at Midhurst in Sussex where I took leave in order to visit her. She was a pitiful sight and obviously dying of cancer. There was little that they or anyone could do for her and I felt a great deal of remorse that I had not given her more of myself throughout her life. I had left home at fifteen and basically parted company with her from then on. Even the short fifteen years that I had spent at home, I had given her nothing but trouble. She passed away in August and was buried at Bognor Regis. She had not had a happy life in any way and was only in her mid - fifties.

MMS 1681 was provided with a new 1st Lieutenant, this time, a young R.N. Lieutenant who was quite efficient and a great change from the previous RNR Lieutenant. We continued with our mine hunting exercises and experiments for the remainder of the year, by which time I had been informed that the MMS was to be paid off and replaced by a brand new in-shore minesweeper being constructed at Samuel White's, Cowes, Isle of White. She was to be H.M.S. Aveley and fitted with all the latest mine hunting equipment I would be required to go to the boatyard in early February, to supervise her completion and accept her on behalf of the Admiralty. So on 4th February I proceeded to Cowes.

At Cowes I had to find my own accommodation whilst Aveley was being completed, there being no Naval establishment on the Island, and found comfortable board in a private home. When ready, the ship had to be seaworthy and all equipment tested and checked. My new crew was appointed and drafted to the ship as soon as the accommodation was ready and we soon began to settle down and to start working the ship up to seaworthy, fighting and minesweeping efficiency. As soon as we were ready, we took her to Portsmouth where we were attached to H.M.S. Vernon the shore establishment for torpedoes, ASDICs and all SONAR equipment and which contained all the experts in these fields. They helped us and trained us in the new equipment until by 21st March 1954 we were proficient enough to re-join our squadron in the Firth of Forth and duly returned – the pride of the squadron and somewhat more capable of pinpointing mines. Exercises, as before, continued though not without breaks.

In the early part of summer 1954 I was sent on a very interesting mission, quite unique for the R.N. From the Firth of Forth, I was to take my ship to Moray Firth, Inverness and through the Caledonian Canal to the Firth of Clyde for exercises and return. This was an extremely interesting trip through the very narrow canal and lochs to Fort William and out to the Atlantic Ocean to the other side. I have some recollection that I had a slight collision with the bank in a narrow part of the canal but no serious damage resulted and the incident passed without serious further enquiries. Not so in

H.M.S. Aveley

July when we paid a visit to Whitby North Yorkshire. This was a good will visit to let the public see something of their Navy. We arrived on Friday of the August Bank Holiday Weekend (the first weekend in August at that time). Whitby Harbour was, and is, small for a warship in which to moor. The water at low tide was shallow and insufficient to allow Aveley to swing. It was therefore necessary for the ship to moor between two buoys by arrangement with the Harbour Master. This was successfully done and the ship was the centre of attraction for the weekend. It was necessary for us to depart on the Sunday afternoon in order to clear the Harbour for the town

Regatta to take place on August Bank Holiday Monday. Duly at 4pm. we prepared to sail. The 1st Lieutenant was in charge aft whilst I could control forward from the bridge. I gave the order to let go aft and when this was done, attempted to swing the stern to port in order that I could come astern, and then move forward bringing the bow to port so that the stern would swing between the two buoys whilst I moved forward. Alas the manoeuvre did not go according to plan. I moved astern as planned, but as I put the wheel to port and moved forward, the stem swung in over the buoy we had just left. The ship juddered and came to a grinding halt. Try as I may, moving my engines slowly one way and then the other, there was no way I could extricate myself from this position. Eventually divers were sent for but they weren't able to do anything either. They tried until dark but it appeared that my propeller shaft had become entangled with the mooring chains of the buoy and that heavy machinery would be required to dislodge them or they would have to be cut free. We remained in this position overnight until divers returned with more equipment at dawn to try again. They eventually managed to free us by midday by which time their regatta had been somewhat disrupted. We were glad to be free, without, as far as we could tell, any serious damage having been done to the propellers or shafts. We made our way back to base where I was subsequently ordered to attend an official board of enquiry into the matter in full dress of sword and medals etc. The board decided that it was not a case warranting court martial but that I was guilty of hazarding my ship and was to be – and was - reprimanded by the Captain of the base. Oh well - I don't think it had any serious effect on my future career.

In early October, Prince Philip, Duke of Edinburgh had official duties to carry out at Dunfermline and it was the intention that he would come to Port Edgar, cross the Firth of Forth by Naval Launch and proceed from Rosyth by car. On the due date, the weather was not good and the sea choppy. I was told to be in readiness to take him across if necessary. It did become necessary and Aveley was quite ready. At the appointed hour, 4pm, the jetty was alive with Captains, Commanders and others, my gangway ready with the piping party and myself at the head to greet him on board. When he arrived and had completed introductions, he was piped on board and I took him up to the bridge, immediately letting go and sailing. We had a pleasant journey across, chatting about various Naval matters. He had cars waiting on the jetty opposite and I had to wait for him to return so that I could bring him back again. This happened around 7pm. He enjoyed his little trip and thanked me, particularly for the bump I gave him coming alongside. Trying to be clever I came in fast, intending to pull the ship up by both engines full astern, slightly misjudged and hit the jetty. No damage sustained, all was well. Later the Prince sent me a signed photograph of himself to hang in our wardroom and I sent him a large photograph of

Aveley asking him to sign it for me, which he did.

By January 1955, my two years with the 51st MMS would be up and myself due for relief. Accordingly in November my next appointment arrived which was not one for which I was able to show any enthusiasm. I was appointed as

Duke of Edinburgh on Bridge

Barrack Guard Officer, R.N. Barracks Chatham from 22nd November - not being due for any leave, I had to say fair well to Aveley. It had been an interesting, enjoyable but not exactly exciting commission.

A SHORE APPOINTMENT - R.N. BARRACKS CHATHAM

This was something about which I knew very little. Almost all of my service since 1934 had been spent at sea, which was where I wanted to be anyway. I could not imagine of what their lordships were thinking to appoint me as barrack guard officer. I was the least likely person, I would have thought, but perhaps they were trying to further my career.

My duties in the barracks would be: complete responsibility of the security, responsibility for the discipline of all ratings in the barracks and to have a guard of 100 men, train them and handle them on all ceremonial occasions, including the weekly divisional parade of the whole barracks every Friday. Further, I was the mail officer or, if you like, post-master general of the barracks. I did not feel that I could handle this and also go off ashore home at 5pm daily. In fact I was somewhat frightened of the whole prospect. I decided therefore that it would be better for Thelma and the children to move back to their own home at Southbourne and I would visit them at weekends i.e. Friday evening until Monday morning. The alternative would be to find furnished accommodation in Chatham or Rochester; not an exactly palatable place to live, especially with myself in a job unsuited to me. We moved down from Kirkaldy back home before Christmas. I sold our little Austin Ruby saloon and bought a larger Austin model in view of the mileage I was likely to be making each weekend from now on.

Thelma was now pregnant again. This had happened the previous summer and our fourth baby would be due in March 1955. This I think was another reason for my preference for her returning to her own home. I felt perhaps that I could not cope with family problems as well as this job and that the two would be better separated.

Life at the barracks was most uninteresting. I would strut around, dressed in uniform, boots and black gaiters, shouting at every one I could: "put your cap on straight", "pick up at the double", "salute when you pass an officer" etc.. I had a gunner (commissioned warrant officer) to assist me – a valiant chap to whom all these duties were second nature. A lot of time was spent with my guard drilling, inspecting, marching, rifle drill etc. They looked very smart in their short white gaiters.

Every Friday was divisions. The barracks was divided into four divisions, some 2000 men I suppose, so each division consisted of 500 men. All were dressed in their best uniform at 9am and fell in on parade, officers with swords and medals. The officers would inspect each of their divisions, correct their dress where necessary and generally make sure they were smart. Meanwhile, I would assemble my guard, inspect them and march them onto the parade ground. Divisional Officers would report their divisions ready for inspection to the commander when appropriate so that by 9:30 the whole parade was formed and the commander would report to the commodore. All officers not on parade assembled on the parapet overlooking the parade with the Commodore and Commander. The Padre would first hold a short service and this would be followed by the Commodore inspecting one of the divisions with the Royal Marine Band playing appropriate military music. It was all inspiring for me, looking up at the assembled officers on the parapet, some thirty feet above the parade ground. The guard was always inspected and I was in front to shout the necessary orders. After the inspection was completed and the Commodore returned to the parapet, came the march past, led by the Guard. For this the Guard had to be manoeuvred into two parallel lines, 50 men to each line with arms at the slope and my sword, unsheathed and held vertical. I always tried my best to shout the orders loud and clear so that not only my Guard could hear them but the whole parade. Unfortunately I tried too hard or was too nervous for the word "Guard" would emanate loud and clear but the next part perhaps "slope arms" would come out as only a squeak - most embarrassing. It must have been nerves and lack of self-confidence. Fortunately the Guard knew what orders were coming, whether they could hear me or not, so the drill went according to plan. We then began the march past, from one end of the parade to the other with a sharp "eyes-right" on passing the saluting base when my sword was smartly brought from its vertical position up in line with my nose and swiftly down to the point facing the ground, about six inches from the ground. This was the sword salute and the original position was resumed in the reverse order on my command "eyes-front". All of this was not me at all really but I made the effort, for that was my duty. The Commander in Chief, Nore, a full admiral, lived in admiralty house adjacent to the Royal Naval Barracks. My Guard also became the Commander in Chief's Guard on those occasions he needed one. Perhaps for visits by foreign dignitaries or by senior officers of foreign Navies or even Admirals from the board of admiralty. I well remember parading the Guard for, and being inspected by, Lord Louis Mountbatten when he was 1st Lord of the Admiralty. The routine was similar to that for Friday divisions except that it did not normally take place on the parade ground but outside Admiralty House with far less if any onlookers. It was much less foreboding.

I had joined R.N. Barracks, Chatham on the 22nd November 1954 when, as I mentioned earlier Thelma was pregnant. Our fourth child was born 7th April 1955, this time a son. I was so pleased, not just for myself but also for Thelma who had so desperately wanted a son after three daughters. We counted our blessings with three lovely daughters and now a son to complete the family. Though I was not quite so pleased that he was born late on April 7th, just two days after the end of the tax year, so that I missed a whole year's tax rebate on the allowances due for an additional child. I remember I was home at the time of Jonathan's birth, probably on Easter leave. Thelma went into the local nursing home on the 6th and her mother was already down from Liverpool in anticipation of the event and ready to take over care of the children. On the morning of the 7th at about 8 am I had a telephone call from the nursing home. It was the doctor to tell me that we had a son, perfectly healthily but there were complications with the birth and that although there was no need for me to be unduly concerned, Thelma had had a bad time but was now resting peacefully. Later, much later, I discovered what an understatement this was. It appears that after the birth, Thelma had had a bad haemorrhage and had lost a tremendous amount of blood. There was no doctor at hand to give immediate attention and although one was quickly summoned, little he could do as the nursing home had no facilities. First thoughts were to transport Thelma by emergency ambulance to Portsmouth, but this was abandoned mainly because Thelma had no desire to return to St. Mary's Hospital after her experiences there with the birth of Julia. The doctor quickly arranged for a supply of blood to be sent from Portsmouth to Emsworth which arrived with ambulance sirens screaming because of the emergency. Meanwhile Thelma, whilst unconscious could hear the nurses around her, quite panicking and shouting "her pulse is weakening, it's going, it's going." The ambulance arrived in the nick of time and the doctor immediately set to work. Meanwhile, at home, I was quite unaware of all that was going on. In the evening, normal visiting hours, I called to see Thelma and our new baby. I was handed the baby at the foot of the stairs and asked to take him up. What I did not know, was that Thelma had not even seen the baby up to this point. When I saw her, she looked tired and strained and very disappointed that she was not showing her baby to me. Rather a thoughtless act by the nursing home staff. From here on, Thelma slowly but surely regained her strength. She remained in the nursing home for over two weeks before she was strong enough to return home but what a near thing this had been.

Meanwhile, Thelma's mother had looked after the children with excellence to the extent that Karen, now little more than two years old, accepted her as her own mother and at first appeared to have forgotten Thelma when she returned. Perhaps it was jealousy at the fuss being made of the new baby which had replaced all the fuss previously made of her as the youngest. I had returned to Chatham to continue with my duties and resumed again my regular weekend visits. In a few days Thelma was able to gather up the reins once more and take over allowing her mother to return home and care for her father - not in the best of health.

In February 1956 the commander of the barracks was relieved at which time, as was customary, he wrote his report on me. I was somewhat surprised to read that in spite of the difficulties, I had kept the security of the barracks sound, that I was always smart and, above all, an asset to the barracks. You could have fooled me! The new Commander was a Dudley Davenport with whom I had served in Sheffield – a Lieutenant in those days. We got along very well and it was probably on his recommendation that I received my next appointment as Commanding Officer of H.M.S. Fenton - a ton class minesweeper. After exactly two years to the day, my time at the barracks was up. I could not have been more thankful or relieved to know that I was to be relieved of these duties. My relief was appointed and took over from me on 23rd November. I was now on leave awaiting my next appointment which did not come before Christmas enabling me to spend some time with my family. During January of 1957, my next appointment came, to H.M.S. Fenton.

H.M.S. FENTON

H.M.S. Fenton to which I was now appointed to assume command was a minesweeper belonging to the 108th minesweeping squadron in the Mediterranean. She was reasonably new, having been completed in August 1955. These ships had a displacement of around 400 tons and around 160ft in length. The engines were two diesels and speed of 15 knots. The complement was Captain - a Lieutenant Commander or Senior Lieutenant, 1st Lieutenant, two Sub-Lieutenants with usually some Midshipmen under training and a crew of approximately 30. As minesweepers there was no steel in the vessels, no portholes and they were built of glass reinforced plastic (GRP). This would be a most interesting command to which I

H.M.S. Fenton

looked forward with great eagerness. Looking back now, this was probably an opportunity for me for promotion to Commander but I had no such thoughts at the time.

Being another foreign appointment for two years, I had to decide what was best for my now rather enlarged family. They were nicely settled back in Emsworth though I had seen little of them for the last two years other than at weekends. Malta was a lovely place, the Mediterranean climate supreme so what better than to take them with me? That of course was not possible, it would be necessary for me to go first, take up my appointment, find accommodation, then obtain permission from the admiralty. I was not due to take up my appointment until the 1st April during which time arrangements had to be made for my transportation to the Mediterranean and thus gave me time to make all the necessary arrangements for the family. I had to let the home, arrange their accommodation, pending passage etc. After Jonathan was born, we found that our small homely little bungalow was not now large enough to accommodate us. We had a two bedroom bungalow with just a lounge and kitchen for six of us to live. There was for sale a rather nice three bedroom semi-detached house with lounge and dining room on the main Southbourne road, just at the top of the road in which we were living. We sold up and bought it, moving in during the summer of 1956 so were nicely settled in when the time came for letting it in February 1957. We all moved up once more to Liverpool to stay with Thelma's parents. I left by ship early in March on route to Malta, for my new post.

I took over command of Fenton on 18th March 1957. My first duties were to make the official calls: my immediate senior officer, the commanding officer of 108th MSS, a commander who was also commanding officer of another minesweeper H.M.S. Sefton, then Captain Inshore Flotilla, a Captain Walwyn, the flag officer Malta and Commander in Chief Mediterranean at Admiralty house. The minesweepers were organized into two squadrons of eight per squadron (104th and 108th). As a Lieutenant Commander of three years seniority I found myself second in command of the 108th which entitled me to have a black band painted around the funnel. The two squadrons were under the control of the Captain Inshore Flotilla who operated from and was in command of the base ship H.M.S. Woodbridge Haven.

At this time trouble had flared up in Cyprus between Turks and Cypriots. Turkey claimed Cyprus to be theirs. Greece also claimed the Island but it was, as far as we were concerned, British. About three quarters of the population were Greek and one quarter Turkish, living mainly to the North of the island, opposite Turkey. Arms were being smuggled in to the Island from both Greece and Turkey and if the fighting was to be contained it was necessary to prevent such arms from getting through. This was an ideal situation for minesweepers to handle, so the Island was constantly patrolled by minesweepers, about six at a time. Without delay, I soon found my ship dispatched to Cyprus for the patrol.

We normally sailed from Malta in pairs, to relieve two others in Cyprus. The period of patrol was approximately six weeks, followed by a six week break in Malta where normal minesweeping exercises and other social events took place with the occasional visit to other Mediterranean ports. In Cyprus, whilst not on patrol, we were based at Famagusta. Outside of the dock area, men had to be armed at all times and even sports parties escorted by the Army and guarded whilst playing, for the forces were a legitimate target. No leave was allowed but there was an open air cinema on the jetty where films could be projected onto a screen after dark. For the purposes of patrol, the Island was divided into five areas, with one minesweeper allocated to each. The duty was to patrol the area day and night on or near the three mile territorial line and to stop and investigate all vessels within territorial waters to ensure their business was legitimate. Sometimes the weather was splendid, at others it could be frightfully rough and uncomfortable. We were always darkened completely at night, in order that we should not be seen and carried on board, an armed boarding party at the ready. I had quite a happy ship, with an excellent 1st Lieutenant, a Lieutenant Jeremy Stewart and other officers. The crew were well seasoned men, all of whom could and did their job well. Occasionally we would be sent RNVR Midshipmen for training. Again, most of them were responsible young men but sometimes there would be a young tearaway who neither knew nor understood Naval discipline. I fear they had an uncomfortable time in my ship but they probably did not care.

The Flag Officer, Middle-East, flew his flag in Cyprus at Episkopi on the South of the island where he lived in what was known as Admiralty House together of course with his wife. Here was a character the likes of which the Royal Navy have seen few before and probably none since. He was Rear Admiral Tony Miers VC. He had been a submariner during the war in command of submarines and won the Victoria Cross for his daring and often suicidal missions. A man of no fear. He took the social activities of minesweepers under his control, at least the officers' social activities, and always during a minesweepers patrol period he would invite the commanding officer and some of his officers for a weekend at Episkopi, some very long way from Famagusta, over 100 miles. These weekends were full of high-jinx, one had to be very fit to keep up with them. I only ever remember attending once and hated every minute of it but no doubt the younger officers had a thoroughly enjoyable time. I was not popular with Admiral Miers; I felt that I was in Cyprus to do a serious job, not to be playboying around at Admiralty House. When arriving at Cyprus for a period of patrol, I refused to sail my ship round Episcopi bay giving three cheers or whatever to the Admiral but went straight to my destination Famagusta. This would displease the Admiral but I cared little. He was I think the rudest man I have ever known both to the Officers and particularly to his wife, who in fact was a very pleasant lady, Pat by name. On one occasion, I felt it my duty to invite the Admiral and his Wife aboard for lunch to repay him for his hospitality to my Officers. What to give him, which was different? This was the problem. I sent the Chief Steward ashore in Famagusta to see what he could find. He returned with what were alleged to be Quail. I felt this would be a rare delicacy for the Admiral but de-feathered as they were, they looked like thin scraggy blackbirds to me.

Anyway, to no avail, this was to be the main course for our luncheon party. None of us had the faintest idea as to how they should be served but they were to be stuffed and roasted with the appropriate vegetables. On the day of the Lunch Party we duly sent our boat in to bring off the Admiral and his wife after anchoring close in Episcopi bay. Pre-lunch drinks and chit-chat went very well and we took our places for lunch with Pat, the Admiral's wife on my right. First course was served and all was still well until on came the main course - two of these scraggy little birds to each plate. The meat was brown and exceedingly tough, there being more tiny bones than meat. During the conversation, Pat remarked to me that she thought Pigeons made a tasty meal. I did not disillusion her and she may have been far more correct than I

A dinner in the Mess

realized at the time. The remainder of the meal passed without incident but I am quite sure the Admiral and his wife were more than pleased to leave later in the afternoon

Meanwhile, back at home things had moved on. I had found what I thought was suitable accommodation in Sliema. It was the upstairs two floors of a largish Maltese house and seemed to have all that we would require. On the basis of this, Thelma and the children were allocated a passage by air in May. As I would be away on Cyprus patrol at that time, I arranged for a friend, or someone thought of as a friend, to meet them on arrival and take them to the accommodation, giving what other help and advice they could. Thelma and the children, Christine (9), Julia (7), Karen (4) and Jonathan (2), travelled 1st Class by rail from Liverpool to Euston with all their luggage. At Euston they took a taxi to the appointed hotel where the taxi driver just tipped them out onto the pavement with all their luggage, collected his fare and was off. Poor Thelma was distraught with four young children and loads of luggage just left on a busy London Street. She struggled into the hotel somehow, with no help and booked in. From here on, all was well, the naval staff came to her assistance with WRENs to look after the children and they were escorted and helped to a comfortable room for the night. The following morning they were again well looked after following breakfast they were seated in a coach and driven to the airport from which they flew direct to Malta.

What a different story on arrival at Luqa airport. Firstly there was no one to meet them. My so called friend was not there. After some wait Thelma began making enquiries and found someone who knew him and telephoned him. He eventually arrived and got them all into his car but decided he would make a detour and took them all around to his home from where he called his wife to "come and see what I've got here". He then took them to the accommodation and duly left. It was exceedingly hot. Thelma got inside almost exhausted by now. The children were very hot and very thirsty but there was no cold water or drink. The refrigerator, which operated by paraffin, did not work. The beds were on two floors, Karen wouldn't accept any of them and when the covers were turned back, they were clearly full of bugs. In addition they were required to sleep under mosquito nets - to which they were not accustomed. The whole situation was like a very nasty nightmare. I know not how Thelma coped during the following few days, perhaps her own memoirs will tell the story but she eventually contacted the captain's wife Mrs. Walwyn who was most kind and very helpful. A married quarter shortly became available at Hibernia Court — an apartment block containing about 12 flats – all married quarters. The accommodation was sumptuous. Well furnished, comfortable and supplied with everything down to the smallest detail, that was needed both for living and for entertaining. To Thelma it was like heaven. On top of this a daily maid was passed onto her from someone leaving, a young Maltese girl by the name of Melita who was like one of the family. The children loved her.

I returned from Cyprus patrol to a very pleasant situation in Malta. The family were happy. Christine and Julia settled into the Navy school at Verdala - mornings only. Afternoons were spent at one or other of the beaches, swimming and generally enjoying life. Before Thelma had arrived I bought, as a surprise for her, a brand new Morris Minor. Thelma had no driving licence but this was not required in Malta. All I had to do was to teach her to make the car go and leave the rest to fate. Our social activity was great, parties on board one or other of the ships most evenings whilst Melita was happy to baby-sit. This gave Thelma the opportunity of getting to know the other officers of ships in both squadrons so that when Fenton was away on Cyprus patrol she never lacked invitations, after all, she was not only of an eligible age but very attractive with it. She will have many a story to tell of this period in her life! On one occasion, I had the dubious pleasure of organising a families day out on Fenton. The plan was for the families of my own ship's company together with the families of those ships absent on Cyprus patrol to have a grand day out. The Captain's wife would also come, a Mrs. Dalgleish, the Captain of Woodbridge Haven having changed in April 1958. We were to sail from Sliema at 9am around Malta and anchor between Malta and Gozo where all would go ashore for games, racing, swimming, picnic lunch etc.. We sailed at the appointed time and I was proud to have Thelma and the Children on the bridge with me. We anchored well enough and put the passengers and food ashore for all to enjoy. Unfortunately, during the afternoon, a fresh breeze sprang up and was funnelling straight up between the Islands. Fearing that if it worsened my passengers, all women and children, might be stranded ashore and after consultation with my 1st Lieutenant, I decided that I ought to bring them all back on board so my boat was sent backwards and forwards to do this. On board, there was little I could do to entertain these ladies and children so felt the only course was to weigh anchor and return to Sliema which we did at 4pm and so ended a rather disastrous day which could have been so very different.

Thus life went on, approximately six weeks away from Malta on Cyprus patrol followed by a six week very pleasant break back in Malta with the odd cruise to one or other on the Mediterranean ports not too far distant from Malta. One would never want this happy life to end but end it must in one way or another.

During 1958 the government of the U.K. reached the conclusion that the country was spending more on defence than it could afford or indeed than was necessary.

Accordingly it was decided that cuts would have to be made in the armed forces, the Navy

On the beach in Malta

taking its full share. Volunteers were called to take early retirement in return for a substantial gratuity, pension earned to date and any help that was necessary to resettle into civilian life. I had to give this matter serious consideration I was now approaching the age of forty and unless I was to be promoted to the rank of Commander would have to retire at the age of 45. Furthermore, I felt I would be able to settle into a suitable occupation far better and more easily at 40 than I would at 45. Added to this, I had a wife and young family who had and were only seeing me occasionally. I was not one of them and it was unfair for Thelma not to have a husband or the children a father. Further promotion was unlikely perhaps because of my age but more so because I had failed to get on socially with the admiral in Cyprus or the Captain of minesweepers in Woodbridge Haven. I was not and never would be a socially oriented character, nor would I attempt pleasantries with any senior officer in order to court promotion. I was in the Navy to do a job to the best of my ability which I did at all times and no more. On this basis I applied for early retirement and had no doubt that it would be accepted as it was.

My relief as commanding officer H.M.S. Fenton was appointed in October 1958 arrived to take over in November and on the 15th I was relieved of my command - sadly. Arrangements were made for myself and the family to fly home on the 16th, so after a farewell lunch by the commanding officers of the remaining minesweepers and packing up our married quarters at Hibernia house, we made our way to the airport and without further incident flew back to the U.K. the end of a very pleasant commission and in fact of a very pleasant twenty five years.

.

Printed in Great Britain
by Amazon